safar

Muslim Women's Stories of Travel and Transformation

Sarah Malik

Illustrated by
Amani Haydar

EXPLORE

contents

Contributors

Yassmin Abdel-Magied

Yassmin Abdel-Magied is an Australian writer and speaker. A recovering mechanical engineer and award-winning social advocate, she has published three books with Penguin Random House including two middle grade novels which she is now adapting for screen.

Born in Sudan and London-based, Yassmin has also contributed to dialogue on the Sudan revolution protest movement. You can follow her on Twitter @yassmin_a, Instagram yassmin_a or Facebook @YassminAbdelMagied.

Aliya Ahmad

Aliya is a racial and economic justice media campaigner who is passionate about increasing the representation of diverse spokespeople from grassroots movements in mainstream media. Born in London and raised in Vietnam, Aliya Ahmad has lived in Kuwait, Malaysia, Pakistan, and Australia. You can follow Aliya on Twitter @_aloo_gobi.

Contributors

Aisha Al-Adawiya

Born in 1944 and based in New York, Aisha Al-Adawiya is the founder and Chair of Women in Islam, Inc., an organisation of Muslim women which focuses on human rights and social justice. She is a former program administrator at the Schomburg Centre for Research in Black Culture in Harlem. You can follow her on Twitter @aaladawiya or Instagram @aaladawiya.

Margari Aziza-Hill

Margari Aziza-Hill is a California-based writer and the co-founder and executive director of the Muslim Anti-Racism collaborative. She has been published in the 2018 book *How to Fight White Supremacy* among other publications. She has a Master's degree in Islamic

history of Middle East and Islamic Africa from Stanford University. Her research includes anti-colonial resistance among West Africans in Sudan during the 20th century and the criminalisation of Black Muslims. You can follow her on Twitter @Margari_Aziza or Facebook @Margari.Aziza.

Dr Susan Carland

Dr Susan Carland is an academic, author, and social commentator based in Melbourne, Australia. She is currently a Discovery Early Career Research Award (DECRA) fellow and a Churchill fellow in the Faculty of Arts at Monash University. Her first book was *Fighting Hislam: Women, Faith and Sexism*. You can follow her on Instagram @susancarland.

Farah Celjo

Farah Celjo is a television presenter, editor, recipe writer and avid traveller who 99% of the time plans travel around a meal. She is passionate about food, travel, running and telling stories. You can follow Farah on Instagram @farahceljo.

Contributors

Tasneem Chopra

Tasneem Chopra is a cultural consultant, diversity trainer, writer and speaker. She was recently appointed the inaugural Ambassador for Women of Colour, Australia and in 2020, awarded an Order of Australia Medal for her efforts in championing

diversity. Tasneem has been named an 'Anti-Racism Champion' by the Australian Human Rights Commission. You can follow Tasneem on Twitter @TasChop, Instagram @tassafierce and Facebook @tasneemchopraccc.

Zenith Irfan

Zenith Irfan was the first woman to scale Pakistan's mountainous regions on her motorbike at the age of twenty. She inspired the film *Motorcycle Girl* and is based in Lahore, Pakistan. You can follow Zenith on Facebook @zenithirfan.zi, Twitter @zenithirfan, Instagram @zenithirfan or via her YouTube channel @zenithirfan.

Nadia Jamal

Nadia Jamal is a former senior journalist with the Sydney Morning Herald. She is the author of the award-winning book *Glory Garage: Growing up Lebanese Muslim in Australia* and *Headstrong Daughters: Inspiring stories from the new generation of Australian Muslim women*. She is also a qualified lawyer and currently works as a compliance specialist at a global bank.

Nora Musa

Nora Musa is a foreign language teacher trainer who has travelled to over 41 countries. Born in Birmingham, UK, raised in diverse London and hailing from a mixed African heritage has inspired Nora to develop an early interest in culture. She loves storytelling and has had articles published on race, culture and identity. She uses social media to share stories and hopes to inspire other solo female travellers to get out there and see the world. You can follow Nora on Instagram @womancrossingborders.

Contributors

Dr Umber Rind

Dr Rind is a doctor working in anti-racism health advocacy. She is a First Nations Badimaya Yamatji and Pakistani woman, based in Australia. You can follow Dr Rind on Twitter @UmberRind or Instagram @umberrind.

Raidah Shah Idil

Raidah Shah Idil is a Malay-Australian author. She was born in Singapore and raised in Sydney, Australia. She has worked in Amman, Jordan and now lives in Petaling Jaya, Malaysia with her husband, three children and mother-in-law. Raidah loves noodle soup, ginger tea and dreams of uninterrupted sleep. You can follow Raidah on Twitter @raidahshahidil or via her website raidahshahidil.com.

Sarah Malik

Introduction

When I first received the brief for this book, I was incredibly excited. Diverse travel stories! Yes!

I grew up in the western suburbs of Sydney, Australia in a working-class immigrant Muslim Pakistani household. Reading was my outlet into the wider world and travel journalism especially gripped me. The idea of being a foreign correspondent, travelling the world and writing, felt like the epitome of power and freedom. But travel to distant climes (besides Pakistan) seemed unlikely, even fantastical. This bind, like anything that was unrealistic, seemed to intensify my longing for travel.

So, instead I read newspapers and travelogues. I devoured the work of Muhammad Asad, formerly Leopold Weiss, the intrepid European writer who converted to Islam, was a translator of the Qur'an, and travelled by foot and camel through the Middle East and Pakistan as a foreign correspondent in the early 20th century. His swashbuckling adventures through epic desert storms and scrapes with authorities, interviewing political figures and opening dialogue between cultures through storytelling, thrilled me. Except Asad was male and white, two things I wasn't.

My life was vastly different to the lush vistas of many writers I read for whom the world seemed to be open and accessible. A lot of this writing was formulated in the context of conquest and empire and needed to be swallowed with a filter. There was another name for 'travel' into communities that cannot reciprocate the intrusion: western imperialism.

Travel and adventure have traditionally been the preserve of the wealthy and privileged. White men got the adventure and the rest of us had to serve them – either as underlings of Empire or as supportive bystanders ironing their socks and taking care of home and hearth before they set off. It's a tenor mirrored in most western travel narratives. None of the people whose stories I read were Muslim women. We were talked about and condescended to in these narratives but we could never return the favour and cast our eyes on those who studied us.

Introduction

This book is inspiration for those who want to see new travel stories. It is structured so that, as a reader, you can choose your own journey through these stories and dip in and out as you choose. Many of the stories in the Islamic tradition revolve around the idea of journey and this journeying usually has a theme of spiritual awakening. One of the key features of this external journey is that it acts as a mirror and precursor to the more important revolution within and is a metaphor for the shift in the inner landscape.

In the Islamic tradition, when Hajar, a Black woman, the second wife of Ibrahim, is cast out of her home with her child Isma'il, it is during her journey in the desert that she experiences the miraculous. Marginalised by society and kin, she runs into the desert begging God for assistance. As she sinks into despair, water gushes forth, creating the well of Zam Zam. Hajar's journey of trusting in God ('tawakkul' in Arabic) rather than man for her survival is replicated by every Muslim in the obligatory rites of Hajj, where pilgrims walk in Hajar's footsteps.

Hajj is the greatest pilgrimage in the world, a focal point for millions of Muslim travellers across the globe. It links the past, present and future ummah or community of Muslims across space and time. Hajar's faith is also remembered in the holiday of Eid al-Adha, the Feast of the Sacrifice, commemorated at the conclusion of Hajj. Other notable women include the prophet Muhammad's wife, the worldly Khadija who oversaw a business enterprise whose agents travelled extensively on her behalf. There was also 8th-century Sufi mystic Rabia al-Adawiya, now buried in Jerusalem, who roamed freely during her life preaching divine love.

These are women who journeyed deep within themselves to live a fully realised life.

In honour of these women, this book amplifies the trail-blazing women of today: Muslim women who are changing the game and creating new narratives. Many of them also speak of expansion, and of sources of help and generosity experienced during a life on the road. A dozen incredible women share their stories, including Zenith Irfan, one of the first women to motorbike through Pakistan's mountainous borderlands at the age of 20. There's Yassmin Abdel-Magied who worked on remote oil rigs in Western Australia at 21. I also interview Aisha Al-Adawiya, a social justice pioneer, who grew up as an African American woman in segregated Alabama, moved to New York as a teenager and later converted to Islam after being moved by the words of Malcolm X.

Some of the greatest spiritual teachers experienced revelation and transformation in deserts, mountains and the wilderness. Journeying alone into the world was a cradle for their despair and desolation and also the spark for inspiration and transformation. It is my hope that Muslim women and girls too can enjoy the self-actualisation and spiritual wonder that journeying can offer. Whether that's on a mountaintop overseas, an awe-inspiring natural environment close to home or connecting with their roots and travelling back to their families' origins. This book deliberately includes Muslim women of different walks of life and affiliations, exploring everything from travelling with a disability, travelling as a mother, to travelling as an Indigenous person and as a child of immigrants. It's filled with inspirational stories and loads of practical tips on everything from how to travel on a budget, how to navigate airport security, how to travel solo and how to embrace a 'traveller's mindset' wherever you are.

Many children of immigrants now live and have taken positions within countries that once ruled over their ancestors. Globalisation, migration and the internet have reshaped relations between the west and formerly colonised countries. Many of the women I speak to note the tension of how they have been both shaped by discrimination but also fortified by the privilege of their western passport. I explore this tension, as well as the difficulties of travelling without male or white privilege and how the spectre of sexual violence is weaponised to curtail women's freedom.

Some women face a double bind: experiencing both the virulent impacts of Islamophobia and patriarchy. We are told that a woman's place is at home, safe from a hostile world. But a world unused to women as free agents reinforces a cycle. If there's no safe space made for women, we must forge it ourselves, sometimes at great risk. On a lower scale, I definitely have echoes of gossipy aunties haunting my consciousness, casting travelling alone as somehow morally scandalous. 'Oh, the things you will get up to if left to your own devices!' seemed to be the message of my youth. But that is also perhaps my point: the things to get up to!

This book is a subjective travel memoir centering my own experiences and that of the individual women featured from a diversity of age, race, class and cultural backgrounds. Due to word count and my own limitations as an English-speaking westerner based in Australia during COVID, it offers only a snapshot of the views and experiences of individuals and is not intended as a definitive catalogue of Muslim life or experience which spans the diversity of over a billion people worldwide.

At its heart, this book explores the spiritual and sensual delight of travel and journeying. To travel is to enjoy the luxury and pleasure of living fully in the world. Many of the women interviewed did not grow up with this privilege but instead claimed it as their right. As the spectre of COVID kept us in our homes and as the climate crisis places our natural landscapes increasingly at risk, it is even more urgent to appreciate, honour and take care of our world. This book hopes to offer a counter-colonial approach to travel, now and into the future, with new storytellers offering respect to the traditional Indigenous owners, environments and cultures, as a form of profound gratitude for this precious inheritance.

This book is about women who find themselves in the thick of the world, its politics, narratives, and natural landscapes. It is about how journeys can create revolutions within, and in turn, without — reshaping our societies and reframing them to work for us.

Saying yes to travel is an act of saying yes to life. It is political. It is a way of laying claim to space, of saying this too, this world, also belongs to me.

1
Adventure

The Road is Calling

Adventure
The Road is Calling

When I was a 26-year-old cadet journalist, I went on a trip for a travel story that I soon understood why no one else in the office wanted. It involved climbing up South-East Asia's highest peak, Mount Kinabalu, a detail I must have missed or underestimated.

'I think it's like the Blue Mountains,' the newsroom travel editor told me, gesturing vaguely with her hands. 'And don't worry, you don't have to do it. You can just do the thermal spa on the ground level instead,' she assured me. I remembered this when I was slipping on rocks sliding up a massive Malaysian mountain at dawn, wondering how I got myself into this.

Mount Kinabalu is in Kota Kinabalu, Borneo, in the state of Sabah, Malaysia, about a two-hour flight from the capital Kuala Lumpur. It stands 4095 metres (2.5 miles) above sea level. Climbing it requires a two-day 17-kilometre (10.5-miles) trek. The other journalists were all men who had been training for months.

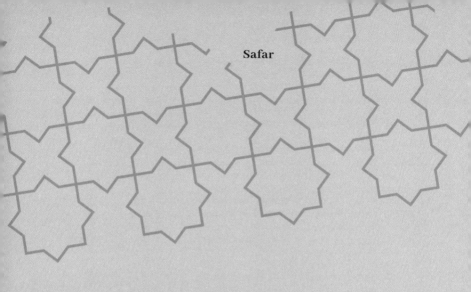

We started Day One at 8am at Ground Zero, ready to scale a 6-kilometre (4-mile) trail of steep steps and large rocks. We made it to the basecamp cabins early that night where we bunked down to rest, before arising at midnight for the second tranche climb. At 2.30am, I looked at the trail to the peak, the miles still above me, illuminated by the twinkling trail of climbers' headlights crawling to the summit. It was dark and freezing cold but I had discarded my thermals and was sweating from the climb.

My body ached, and my heart hammered with panic.

But soon we ascended through the wispy white clouds into the dawn sky. At the summit I breathed with relief and surveyed the view: horizons of mountains, valleys and clouds.

Looking back I still can't believe I actually climbed a whole freaking mountain. I am the type of person that finds a few flights of stairs arduous. I'm so scared of heights that I avoid looking over the railings in shopping centres and refuse to live in a building higher than four levels. But this challenge invited itself into my life and I decided to meet it. There was something special about doing something so physically challenging, something I was deeply terrified of and had no idea I could do. I felt my chest hammering away in fear as my body was stretched in ways I had no idea it could be stretched. Would I do it again? No. Was I proud I managed to complete the climb without being seriously injured? Yes.

***

Testing limits is what motivates Zenith Irfan. She made headlines in Pakistan when she became the first woman, at 20 years old, to travel and blog about riding her motorbike across the country, including the mountainous areas near Pakistan's borders. She became an overnight celebrity, a television presenter and even inspired a movie. For Zenith, risk and reward are both part of the thrill of travel, of testing your boundaries in the wild.

'This is a question everyone keeps on asking me, "Weren't you scared, weren't you scared?"' the 26-year-old tells me.

'The thing is, when you're passionate about something, when your dream is there and you are living that dream, the fear takes a back seat.'

For Zenith, like a lot of travellers who do hugely adventurous things, the steps she took to accomplishing them were small. She was born in Sharjah in the United Emirates. When her father Dr Major Irfan Kabeer died suddenly from a heart attack, the family was forced to return to Pakistan's northern city of Lahore when she was a teen. Losing her father at a young age made her want to rediscover who he was and what mattered to him. After her father died, she discovered through pictures his love of bikes and later his dream of riding the country on a motorcycle. It was a dream that he was never able to fulfil as the responsibilities and realities of family, work and life intervened.

'It's very unfortunate that people have to run after security, job and money. They have to get married at a certain age but are never given the freedom to live their lives or their dreams,' Zenith tells me. 'There was this thing in my head that kept telling me, 'Dreams don't die.' Even if a man dies, the dream continues to live on and I can breathe life into my father's dream by taking this trip for him. All the circumstances were falling into place and the universe eventually pushed me to take that first step.'

That first step was learning how to ride a bike so she and her brother could move around the city. The family lived in Cantt, near Lahore airport, and the city lacked effective public transport. Zenith started riding her bike to university. She was the only female student that did so, raising eyebrows.

In the beginning she was nervous and would only ride through city traffic accompanied by her brother. She gradually gained the confidence to go herself. When she was 19, she joined a desert biking event in Cholistan, in Southern Punjab, with her brother. It was an event she found out about through online motorcycle forums. It was a testosterone-fuelled desert rally on the border of India.

She went to the rally excited to meet fellow bikers, people who loved riding as much as she did but what she found dispirited her.

Zenith Irfan

The mostly male bikers at the rally told her she shouldn't be riding, warning her she could be harassed or injured. Zenith felt her heart drop. Later one biker named Irfan reached out and told her and her brother that he supported and admired her. The pair became fast friends. Irfan Bhai, as Zenith calls him, would become her mentor. He lent her his 125cc Honda and helped Zenith and her brother accomplish their first rides into the Khunjerab pass in 2015, an over 4000-metre (2.5-mile) mountain pass in the Karakoram mountains on Pakistan's northern border with China. Zenith and her fellow travellers spent 20 days on the road from Lahore, riding through Islamabad, the Grand Trunk Road, Naran, Babusertop, and Skardu.

'When you're on the motorcycle, everything is amplified in terms of beauty and the natural elements. You are exposed to the roads, smog, pollution, dust and rain,' Zenith tells me. Zenith went on to travel through Hunza Valley filled with majestic icy mirror lakes and even skimmed the borders of Balochistan and Afghanistan. She visited remote communities and learned about Pakistani's cultural

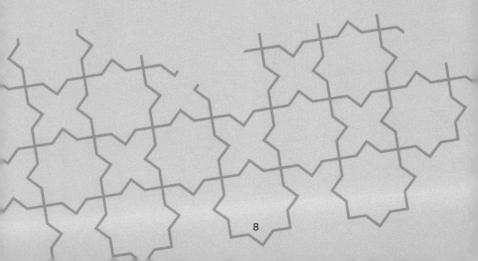

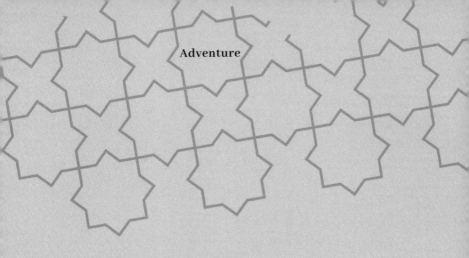

and religious minority groups. Zenith was overwhelmed by the beauty and diversity of the country: 'Some of the places I've been to are very beautiful. Even six years later, I continue to be overwhelmed by the hospitality and by the beauty of Pakistan.'

Despite the warnings from bikers and others, Zenith found riding through the mountains an incredible experience. 'The mountains are actually very safe. Everyone is so hospitable. I never felt unsafe in the mountains. I never felt vulnerable.'

But riding was not without its hairy moments. During a trip through Pakistan's Karkari Lake, Zenith ignored her instinct against riding at night when there is low visibility. Her group had been convinced by their local volunteer guide that it was safe to keep riding. They travelled back with the darkness descending. As they rode across a makeshift bridge, Zenith's motorcycle fell off the bridge. She slipped off the bike and fell into a cold mountainous lake. The horrified guide dove in after her and even saved her bike. 'That was the one time I was literally close to death,' Zenith says.

The apologetic guide took her to his house where his family generously ministered to Zenith. 'I was back on the motorcycle after a day. I did not give up!'

Zenith's advice to young women embarking on adventure is to go for it. 'Think out loud. They have to really stand for themselves and dream big. Be somebody who asks yourself a lot of questions. Do I want this? Do I accept this? Am I willing to put up a fight for this? Don't be scared of society, because society is changing.'

Zenith says the risk-taking and confidence that adventuring across Pakistan taught her has changed her relationship to her life and her work. It made her more assertive in asking for what she wants and prepared to leave situations that don't serve her.

Riding was a reminder that the world was a big place and that one should not hesitate to speak their mind and take a risk. It's a feeling that gave her the courage to take creative control of her new public career when she felt it was moving in a direction she did not feel comfortable with. In those moments of doubt, Zenith would remember being a young girl fearlessly taking on the road with nothing but a dream and enthusiasm. She remembered to hold fast and push back against work that didn't align with her values, knowing the road would always welcome her when she needed freedom.

'If you believe in yourself, there is this drive and spark in your eye that intimidates others, and they know, "We cannot mess with her." But if you don't believe in yourself, you will lose focus.'

Zenith has met naysayers on the road and on social media but they are negligible compared to all of her positive experiences. 'We have minds, we have hearts, and we have goals. There are so many boss ladies out there.'

'You have to eliminate the white noise and be focussed and know what you really want. It's a very difficult journey. It's not easy. It sounds fancy and easy, but it's not. It will be difficult. So, are you ready for the challenge?'

Just like for Zenith, for me, climbing Mount Kinabalu, was about proving to myself I could meet the mountains in my own life and change my own conception of myself as someone who was courageous and brave, who could do things that were completely out of my comfort zone despite being terrified. I do advocate working with the right support, safety precautions and training though!

Safar

Travelling into natural landscapes whether it is diving down into the depth of the sea, hiking in nature, climbing or the rush of adventure sports is an incredible way to test your body and its limits and meet new people. But its greatest power is in slowing down time and helping us appreciate the world in all its incredible grandeur and beauty.

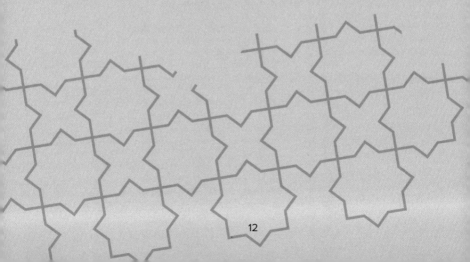

2
Roots

Travelling with Family

Roots
Travelling with Family

For many women I spoke to, one of the first and most memorable travel journeys they remembered taking was going back to their parents' homelands for the first time. As children of migrants growing up in the west, caught between cultures, going 'back' home can be filled with excitement but also confusion and the stress of expectation. Will I fit in? What will I discover about myself? How will it change how I feel about my family, who they are and where they come from, and, by extension, myself?

As a kid I remember being so excited about trips back to Pakistan. I remember lugging way too much hand-carry on Singapore Airlines' flights. Bags filled with packaged chocolate, honey, and beauty products for summer holiday trips to the city where my parents were born: Karachi, Pakistan. I remember the humid air and playing cricket in corridors of the inner-city buildings we lived in, in the working-class Karachi area of Kharadar. Our extended family were not wealthy materially but always generous in spirit and they appreciated the gifts. Electronic goods would be repurposed and hum smoothly after being refitted by a clever street stall vendor and recycled for a second life. It made me appreciate more deeply the material privileges I grew up with that I often took for granted.

For Australian television presenter and editor Farah Celjo, her memories of her first plane trip carry an excitement similar to my own. When she was 15, she travelled back to her mother's hometown of Gorazde, Bosnia, in 2002. She travelled with her mother Fatima and brother, after the sudden loss of her father. The family had not been back for 16 years as Bosnia was ravaged by war in the 1990s. The trio landed in Sarajevo airport to a crowd of excited relatives.

'I was so excited and a little bit nervous,' Farah says of that first trip. As a young girl, Farah was oblivious to her mother's heavy emotions on returning back to her home. 'I was like a kid going to an amusement park. It was all of these sensory experiences. I remember getting into Sarajevo and my mum was sitting next to me on the plane and she was just crying as we were coming into land. It was the first time in 16 years she had been home to see her brothers and sisters. At the airport, all our relatives are hugging my mum and yelling and smiling. It was all these people who knew me, knew my brother, and who hadn't seen my mum in over a decade. They were just hugging us and loving us within the first hours of being in Sarajevo.'

The vibrant celebrity-style welcome was something I was also used to. To my relatives, I was coming from a country and people they saw only in movies and usually after years of minimal contact. There was no Skype, WhatsApp or social media in the 1990s. Letters would be intermittent and my parents would use phone cards for snatches of conversation on bad lines. Like me, Farah was also about to be greeted by language confusion and adjust to the rhythms of a new culture. But part of the excitement of the journey was in the anticipation. Later as an adult, when I revisited the streets of Kharadar, I marvelled at how far away this all seemed from our life in suburban Sydney. I mused how far away it must have seemed to our relatives who wondered about what life was like in Australia – an exotic place they only saw on television, represented by bushfires, beaches and kangaroos.

Kharadar was full of life not like our sleepy suburb in Sydney. Kharadar's crowded streets and alleyways teemed with street-wallahs selling their wares. The adhan rang out from the locals mosques. As kids, we lit candles when the lights went out and told jinn stories. We played hide-and-seek on the streets. I remember using squat toilets and bucket showers and waiting for hot water. It made me appreciate where my parents had come from and the sacrifices they had made in immigrating to Sydney to try to give their kids more materially. I loved seeing the country where the colours of my shalwar kameez matched the rickshaws and trucks that were decked out in tassels and fluoro colours. All the food sold in the streets matched the food we ate at home in Australia with some added delicacies. I marvelled at the taste of flavoured ice adorned with coconut, the roasted spiced nuts sold in paper bags on the street. I remember drinking delicious, thick, creamy chai made from

Farah Celjo

buffalo milk and of course the most exquisite fluffy, tender biryani. It's food that I still dream about.

For Farah, the trip to Bosnia also helped her see herself and her own mother Fatima in a different light, as the person she was before she was a mother. For Farah it was a reminder that her parents too were three-dimensional people with their own hopes, dreams and expectations before they immigrated to the west.

'I saw my mum in her element,' Farah recalls as she watched her mother interact with her family in her hometown. 'I saw her relax and be the person that she would often tell me about. The person in those stories, twenty-something years ago, when she was this career woman who dated but wasn't ready to settle down and used to go to the Mediterranean coastline to holiday.'

'I saw her stripped back of all the anxieties she must have faced coming here. The uncertainty of being in a society she didn't know, a society where she was stripped of her language and didn't feel comfortable communicating. And in a place with no memory but that was actually safe and new.'

Each immigrant kid 'return' story is unique, and each person connects with place differently.

For some there is a sense of loss and alienation, a hope that doesn't meet its romanticised expectation. For others there is a sense of piecing together the puzzle of their lives, a rootedness to a history that felt hard to grasp. For me, travelling back to Pakistan as an adult felt like a combination of both.

Roots

Australian author and former journalist Nadia Jamal first went back to Lebanon at the age of 16 to the town where her parents had immigrated from: the northern coastal city of Bakhoun. It was Nadia's first time on a plane. Like me, her parents were working-class immigrants with big families so going back to the homeland with gifts and money was an event that was saved up for with care. 'It was a big trip packing up the family and going back to Lebanon to visit all of the relatives for the first time,' Nadia says.

Nadia's parents had saved for years for the trip. The trip from Sydney to Lebanon for the family of seven cost $30,000 – a small

fortune ten years ago. It was a decision that had not been taken lightly. Nadia says it was a choice for her parents between buying the house next door or making the trip. 'They decided to invest the money giving us a once in a lifetime family experience. That was a big call to make, setting aside the material things and saying: "We want to spend our money on our children meeting their relatives and seeing where we grew up."'

For Nadia, the experience lit a spark for an interest in travel. 'For me travelling is an investment in growing your mind and becoming a richer person. It's often said and I believe it is true: it opens your eyes to the world in a way nothing else can.'

Like Farah's, Nadia's trip was not without cultural confusion. Nadia had absorbed Arabic from Saturday school classes but after being in the country for five minutes, she wasn't prepared for the grilling from relatives about which country she liked more – Australia or Lebanon. 'I remember thinking, why am I being asked this? Do I have to choose? I like them both! But of course, Australia I like first and foremost because it's where I was born and where I see my life.'

For Farah, the funniest clashes were over her clothes from Supre, an Australian chain store aimed at tween girls, full of cheap clothes, in-your-face colours and loud music, featuring all the fashion choices you'll live to regret. 'I came over with outfits from Supre. Like pedal pushers and cropped dresses over cropped jeans. My family were like, "Why are you wearing pants that are too small for you? Boob top? Where are the straps?" My fashion sense seemed wacky but to me I didn't know people who dressed differently to me and that was wacky!' she says with a laugh.

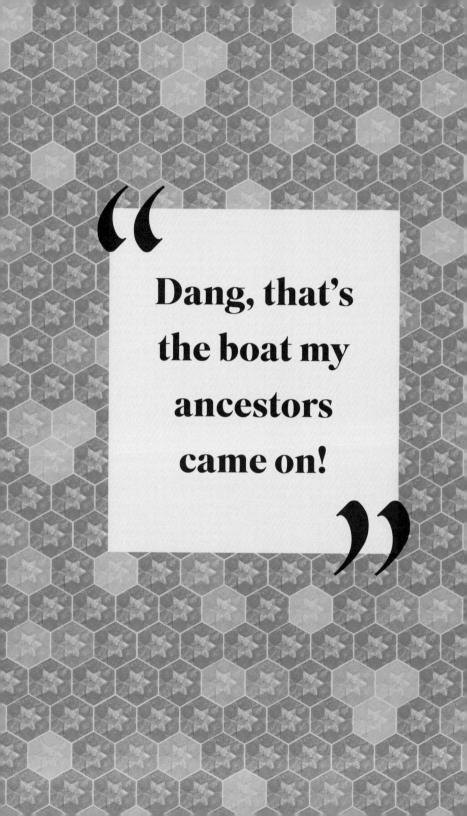

"Dang, that's the boat my ancestors came on!"

For me, the worst faux pas were not in fashion but in language. Tripping over Urdu and Memon, the Pakistani dialect my family spoke, always made me feel shy. I found myself mixing Urdu with English when I couldn't summon the right word. I found that speaking English was paradoxically highly prized, a sign that you were a westerner awash with foreign cash. This prizing of English is something Farah discovered as a teen.

'We were these little Aussie children, just embracing everything and probably a real novelty. I just felt so embraced.'

'I felt super Australian when I went to Bosnia because of my accent. It was probably the first time I actually noticed I had one. I was pretty fortunate because I had spoken Bosnian for the first five years of my life at home before I went to school and learnt English. My accent was terrible and my pronunciation hilarious. All the girls in the town I hung out with were all trying to learn English and I was trying to learn Bosnian. One girl would watch *Friends* and other US sitcoms in the hopes of bettering her English. She would write me these letters in English and send them to me. I'd mark it and tell her what she did not spell right. She got top marks in English at school! She later told me, "It was because I wrote about you and all the things we had done together."'

For Nadia, the trip instilled a lifelong love of Lebanon, a small country where you can travel from one end to the other in under a few hours without traffic. It's a devotion that comes as a surprise even to her. 'I have Lebanese heritage and it's something that I'm proud of. Sometimes I get surprised by how close I feel to it and how emotional I can be about it because I didn't grow up there.'

One of the things I loved about walking through Karachi streets was the sensory difference. The energy and bustle was 24/7 with the fragrant offerings of flower-wallahs my favourite. I loved watching them sell garlands of velvet red roses and jasmine. Both plants sit on my balcony and their heavy perfumes remind me of the flower-wallahs of Pakistan. I remember every kind of delicacy sold on the street including the sweet-wallahs pouring fiery orange jalebis in hot vats of oil.

For Nadia the trip to her parents' homeland provided a similar kind of sensory appreciation. 'There is a level of superficiality to Lebanon that I don't know whether to laugh or cry about. But then there's this special love of life and a buzz and excitement that's quite rare. It is also defined by an obsession with some of the arts — music, dancing and acting. Lebanon draws so many artists from the region. It's as if every second person there tells you they're a singer or an actor. I mean how many performers can one small country have?' she laughs.

For Tasneem Chopra, a cross-cultural consultant based in Melbourne, Australia, her first trip back to her parents' homeland — Zanzibar and Kenya, formerly united as Tanganyika — happened later in life. At 40, Tasneem had what she describes as a mid-life epiphany and decided to return to university to pursue a degree in international development. She also decided to travel to Nairobi, the capital of Kenya, and Stonetown, her father's birthplace, also known as Shangani, in Zanzibar. As a fifth-generation East African with

Tasneem Chopra

Indian roots, Tasneem says the experience travelling to Stonetown gave her an experiential window into how her parents grew up, something that seemed only theoretical until that point. 'It just felt like I was literally transported in time. I felt such a profound sense of "I have been here before" when I walked down the streets.'

Tasneem's first task on arriving in Stonetown in the evening was to see the dhow boats — large vessels that drifted along the magnificent Zanzibari port. There was a model of a dhow boat that sat in Tasneem's parents' living room in Bendigo, an Australian town in country Victoria where she grew up. 'I was told: "This was the dhow boat your ancestors arrived in Africa on."' When Tasneem saw those very boats in person, lazily drifting the harbour in real time, she got emotional. 'It was a magnificent port. When I arrived in Zanzibar on the first evening and went to the port and saw the dhows, I was like, "Dang, that's the boats my ancestors came on!" They are now fishermen's boats because no one migrates to Zanzibar on a boat now. I remember taking a cruise on the dhow that first night and just moseying down the coast.'

Later, Tasneem wandered the stone alleyways, after watching the dhow boats from the shore. The narrow stone paths precluded cars and their traffic and smoke, leaving the cobblestone alleys free for bicycles, scooters and pedestrians. She noticed houses with ancient handmade wooden doors carved with symbols that represented the family's ancestral occupation. Symbols of trees meant the family had been agriculturalists, coins denoted a business history.

Roots

Tasneem was staying at a family friend's beautiful old hotel, converted from a traditional Zanzibari family compound. Each floor in the building featured a self-contained apartment, designed for multigenerational extended families. Tasneem smiled as she noticed her room decked out in Freddie Mercury homage. The iconic Queen lead singer had grown up around the corner from Tasneem's father's family home in Stonetown. The story of how the rock star was a neighbourhood boy was a tale she grew up hearing. The jigsaw started to come together as Tasneem was able to piece together family lore by physically seeing the places her family talked about.

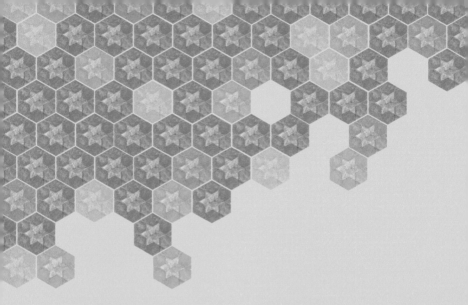

One thing I experienced in Pakistan was also connecting to a sense of my own history. I visited Karachi in 2015 as an adult on my own for the first time. This time, I visited the house of Muhammad Ali Jinnah, the founder of Pakistan. His childhood home, now a museum, is a short walk from my parents' house in Kharadar. It felt like living history to be connected to a person who set in train a series of events that led to me being who I was, here in Australia, a child of immigrant parents who were born just after partition. My family left Pakistan in the late 1970s, first immigrating to the US where I was born, and later to Sydney as economic immigrants, seeking a better life. It was decades after the partition of the Indian subcontinent and the end of the British Raj, and English colonisation of the continent. It felt like Jinnah connected me to a history that was connected to my own trajectory from this land and its political and economic fortunes.

Tasneem felt something similar in her dreamlike tour of Stonetown. A chance meeting with her father's family friend led her to the local cemetery which featured grave stones for multigenerational families.

Roots

Despite the Arabic and Gujarati of the gravestone inscriptions being indecipherable to her, Tasneem knew that this was where her grandparents and even their parents had been buried. As she paid her respects in this ancient cemetery far from her home in Melbourne, she felt connected to something bigger than her: 'It was a really reflective moment and also a moment of doing something that gave me a connection to my roots. It was a beautiful thing. I left feeling I knew they were there and I felt happy at having gone seen them.'

For Farah, the experience of going back to Bosnia, filled as it was with deep emotion for her mother, also changed her relationship to the world and her sense of her own history: 'I feel so connected to a place that I wasn't even born in and that I didn't grow up in. It just felt like the safest space. I felt like I finally understood my family for the first time. When I came home, I said to my mum, "I'm going to live there someday." Ever since then, Bosnia has always been my sanctuary when I visit Europe.'

Safar

For so many of the women I spoke to, their first travel experiences were not for pleasure or leisure but necessity. These early experiences instilled a sense of understanding difference and becoming curious about their own place in the world. Being children of immigrants, the trips back to their parents' homelands, sometimes small towns and villages, allowed them to see a world outside of hotels and major cities.

There was an opportunity to be aware of contrast early on in life and also ponder the existential question of how life could have turned out differently had it been for different circumstances and choices made by their parents. There's also a wonder at how one's life can be shaped by so many forces outside our control. To travel and be able to live within a culture and with extended family members also provided unique vantage points.

For Nadia, being soaked in the culture of Lebanon helped her develop a love for its artistic spirit. For Farah, picking apples in Gorazde orchards while watching her mother connect with her extended family made her see someone so close to her in a whole new light. For Tasneem, visiting ancestral burial grounds provided her with a sense of her own family history. For me, living near the ancestral museum home of the founder of Pakistan helped me unpack some of the political forces that have shaped my family's fortunes and my own life story.

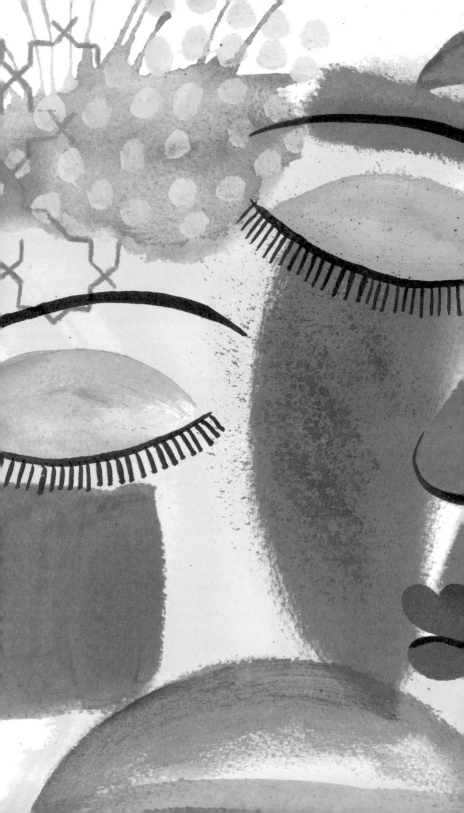

3
Identity

Travelling to Yourself

Identity
Travelling to Yourself

I never feel more Australian than when I am abroad, which is funny because no one else thinks I am Australian. The question 'Where are you from?' is inevitable when I am overseas, and 'Australian' rarely cuts it. People take in my dark skin and ask sceptically, 'Where are you really from?' It's a question I get with depressing regularity in Australia as well, so often that it leaves you questioning yourself too: 'Where am I really from? And where do I belong?'

Paradoxically, when I leave Australia, I ache for the beach and the sand, a café latte, the open space, Medicare and free doctor visits. I long to be able to drive my car on highways and know the routes. I love the opportunity to eat every kind of food from every culture. But when I was growing up in Australia in the 1990s, I often felt stifled by the lack of diversity on screen and in media where I felt like the odd one out.

Identity

The Australian history I learned at school was a 200-year history of English settlers and convicts who arrived on the First Fleet, often bypassing the First Nations history of the continent.

For those of us with mixed or immigrant heritage, travelling can compound those feelings, making us face painful questions from people poking around and judging the authenticity of our identities: too Muslim, or not Muslim enough.

For Dr Umber Rind, a First Nations Badimaya Yamatji and Pakistani woman, travel has unearthed painful memories of not feeling like she belonged anywhere. In the mining town of Pilbara in Western Australia, where she grew up, she copped racist abuse from the white kids. Later as a teen visiting Pakistan, she felt she did not fit in there either. As an adult and medical student in Melbourne, she struggled to find a place within Muslim immigrant communities.

The fraught feelings of identity and safety that a place can conjure up is particularly pronounced for Dr Rind. Her great-grandfather Gulam Badoola arrived in Australia in the late 1890s, recruited from British-colonised India as a cameleer to navigate Australia's deserts. He married Mariam Martin, a Badimaya Yamatji woman. When Mariam passed away in the 1930s, Gulam fled Australia with his four young kids, fearing his children would become part of the Stolen Generations, a state policy of removing First Nations children from their families. He feared they would lose their connection to their identity and religion.

Mariam's kids grew up and got married in India, in what is now known as Pakistan. In the 1950s, Umber's grandfather Numrose decided to return to the land of his birth, the Pilbara, his traditional land. He found work in transport and later brought his Indian-born children. One of them was Dr Rind's dad, who went on to marry a Pakistani woman and had Umber and her two younger sisters.

For Umber, the journey of finding yourself through place starts with becoming unapologetic about who you are and not 'trying' to fit into an identity box others are so keen to put us in.

'Just remember that even though you feel like you're the only one being othered, there's a lot of us,' Umber tells me. 'I think we just need to find each other because I think there is a bit of a tribe we could create here in our home countries. You're not alone in that feeling. Lots of us have gone through that feeling of being othered. Remember you don't owe anybody any special explanations for your identity, especially if you are still working it out.'

As Umber said this to me, I could literally hear myself exhaling.

So other people felt like this too? I asked her how to deal with strangers who were too persistent with questions and comments about your nationality or race, in an intrusive rather than curious way.

'You say what you're comfortable with. I personally am more comfortable with saying I'm a Muslim before Australian. Australian identity is very tricky for First Nations people. You look at the history of colonisation. Not a lot of us like to call ourselves Australian for that reason — what comes with it. So I'm just proud. My identity is: I'm Muslim. I'm a First Nations Muslim woman with Pakistani heritage.

Dr Umber Rind

Aliya Ahmad

I don't speak the languages of my parents. That's okay, too. My advice is, you don't owe people an explanation. '

When overseas, though, an easy answer is sometimes the best option when buying a burger or getting change. She acknowledges the curiosity can be well-intentioned. When the question comes up, Umber will often say: '"Well, we're from Australia." But then they look at us and go, "But what is this?", pointing to the hijab. And I'd say, "Oh yeah, we are from Pakistan too." You don't want to sit there and open up the book of your history to every single person in every shop. You do definitely have to have your easy answer ready.'

Sometimes travel can liberate you from some of your identities, freed from the expectations of how you should behave. Aliya Ahmad was born in London, grew up in Vietnam, studied in Melbourne, and also identifies as queer. Her identity has always been multifaceted. Her Pakistani banker father had a job that kept the family on the move from Asia to the Middle East, and home was always where you made it. This roving childhood made Aliya more open to allowing her identity to shift with place and allowing place to do the same with her.

'Being Muslim, people have an idea about me. Being Pakistani, people have an idea about me. Being queer, people have an idea about me. Those identities often don't intersect neatly. I find that when I am travelling, I can be all of those things at once. All I have to do is bring myself to a country — all of myself.'

'When I'm travelling. I'm just travelling. I'm here to learn from you. My identity becomes the background because I make the foreground where I am. If people ask me about my identity, I share it. But at the same time I can put the intersecting pressures of that identity on the back burner, which is why I love travelling. It is an escape from all the different social pressures. When I'm travelling, I just meet people where they are and they can share as much or as little as they want. I meet people based on who they are rather than meeting people based on different groups.'

In Australia, a country she calls home, Aliya often felt torn by her identities. When she travelled to Russia for the first time after university, she felt free of herself in a place that was completely disconnected from her own history. But she also felt deeply connected to Russian history, as a researcher who had spent a lifetime obsessed with the Cold War and the Soviet Union. Inspired by her high school teacher Sally Painter, who taught by illustrating the places she had travelled, Aliya too wanted a front-row seat to a history she could touch.

'There can be a personal sting when travelling to a place where you see the remnants of a history that excluded you.'

For Aliya, that is going through her parents' city of Karachi and seeing the vestiges of English imperialism, from statues to exclusive country clubs named after white men, places that still exclude women. 'I absolutely love going back to Pakistan – it is amazing – but there is a deeper baggage that comes from people who have been colonised. You feel, "Oh I'm navigating this space, where I would have been subjugated and treated like a lower person."'

Identity

For Aliya, navigating this baggage meant creating an identity different from that of her mother and grandmother who were not granted the luxury and privilege of travelling alone. It was learning from the past to embrace opportunities without fear or guilt. 'For people of colour and also women, you have to carry the baggage of your mother, grandmother and great-grandmother, of being a Muslim woman, and all the expectations of family, as well as colonialism. I find that when you travel sometimes it's like, you're taking the baggage off. And hopefully, for the next generation, maybe that baggage is lighter.'

***

Nora Musa's travels to East Africa were especially transformational in helping her connect to her identity. Born in Birmingham, UK, she grew up in London in a family with mixed heritage: her mother is Egyptian and father is Somali.

Here I speak to Nora about how travelling to East Africa helped her connect with herself and find a sense of peace after losing a loved one.

Tell me about yourself.

When I graduated, I got into investment banking which I really didn't like but I kind of fell into it. I decided it wasn't for me. It was super stressful. It just didn't bring me any joy.

Now I work in teaching English as a foreign language. I taught for a while and then I became a teacher trainer. Education has made me a lot more confident. I think that also has helped me in terms of travelling because as a teacher you've got to be organised, you've got to speak to people, you've got to be confident, even when you're not feeling confident. When I first moved to teaching, I thought I could work abroad because I always had this global outlook. It's less lucrative but teaching gave me more annual leave than when I was in the corporate world. People in my classes are from everywhere: Colombia, Senegal, Indonesia, Spain, Italy. I didn't know much about the culture of Colombia or Mexico, apart from what you see on TV. Meeting these students was just incredible — you learn so much. Things like, there is a mixed ethnic population in northern Colombia, mainly of African descent. I ended up going to South America purely

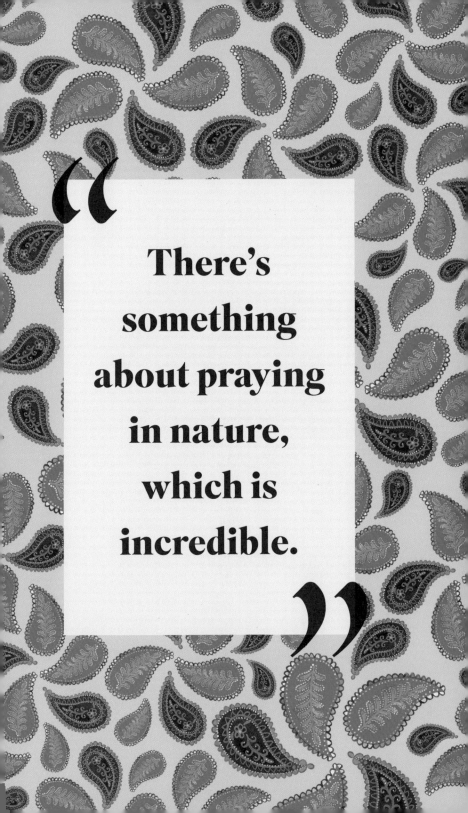

There's something about praying in nature, which is incredible.

because I had been teaching people from there. I wanted to go somewhere new and my family was like: 'Are you crazy? Where is that on the map? Show me!' Teaching has opened the door for me to learn about different cultures and meet people from places I probably would never have visited.

How has travel changed your relationship to your identity?

Identity has always been quite an interesting thing for me. I think it's the same with anyone who has parents from different places and were born in a third place. London is full of people like this. It's not like I'm the only one in a very white village. This kind of not-being-of-one-place, you do have this cultural baggage and you do think about it. As you get older, the idea of, okay, maybe I'm not 100% accepted because I don't speak Somali is there. I can speak Arabic because my mum speaks Arabic and she took us to Egypt a few times when we were kids. But even there I'm darker than the average Egyptian. They look at me and they're like, 'You from Sudan?' Also being a Muslim in the UK, there's that third layer as well. I did feel there were always limitations on what you could do.

How has travel influenced your spirituality?

Senegal is 97% Muslim. It's one of my favourite places. I remember sitting on my own looking at the sea in Senegal's capital of Dakar as people were walking by. This old man climbed up these rocks and he had a milk crate with bottles and he was filling them with

Nora Musa

ocean water. Then this young guy came and sat next to me. He must have been about 17, 18. It's a Francophone country and he's trying to practice his English. He said, 'We are just going to pray.' Prayer time was not in a mosque but in a public place. I found that quite impressive. He proceeded to do his wudu.

I turned around and they put a plastic sheet on the floor in a little corner. I could see there were four rows and each row had four or five people. He asked, 'Do you want to join us?'

I was happy that he asked me, number one. But at the same time I was thinking, 'Where am I going to pray?' It's a public place. I just felt self-conscious about it.

Similarly on an island off the coast of Senegal, the same thing happened. I really wanted to pray. I thought I'll take the ferry to take me back as I'll miss the prayer time. Then people said, there's a mosque right here. They took me around and it was a square. A man said, 'You see that tree. There's a slightly raised bit of ground and there's a plastic sheet.'

There were ladies there. Nobody was staring at me. It was hot and I did my prayer and it was the most wonderful prayer. The tree is giving you shade. You have the breeze that's cooling you down. There's something about praying in nature which is incredible. I don't normally do that. I'm always inside if I pray. Men and women both, they have these little teapots they have for wudu. They will leave their goods and do their prayer in the market.

I just was really impressed by that. It's woven into the everyday life and at the same time they're very accepting. They take Fridays very seriously. Friday, you would think that there's a wedding going on. West African cultures in general like colour. They're not afraid to wear colour. You'll see people in blue, in pink and white and red. On Friday, everyone wears the traditional dress. It's very loose and flowing, almost like a thobe. The women will wear head wraps, and it's just beautiful. People would be dressed in their finest.

Tell us about your first trip to Senegal.

I first went to Senegal in February 2018. My younger brother had just passed away in December. I was supposed to travel a couple of months before that to Senegal. His ill health was accelerating so I cancelled it and my annual leave was due at the time. I thought, I can either postpone it and work or I can travel. So I thought, let me travel. It was also a good time for me to be alone. When you're grieving, sometimes you need to be by yourself. I remember when I got on the plane to go to Senegal and I arrived I felt this thick heat and light. There was something about being in Africa that was rooting for me.

East Africa is my favourite place in terms of being content because I blend in well there. I go to Kenya every year. I've been to Tanzania a couple of times. I went to Ethiopia in 2019 and that was incredible because it's the only country where nobody knew that I was not from there. People kept asking me for directions! I don't speak the local language, Amharic — I speak three words, and that's it. People were surprised when I couldn't speak. I remember being in a cafe. I gave them my order and I was asked: 'Why are you speaking in English?' They asked me, 'Aren't you Ethiopian?', and I said no. They couldn't believe it. I said my father is Somali. It was actually nice walking around and seeing people that looked like you. I remember seeing these two girls and thinking, they have my face and similar features.

I feel content when I'm in what they call sub-Saharan Africa. I just feel that you're not othered as much. I feel people allow the community and faith to be part of the everyday. It's not a big deal to be living with extended families, and they have these compounds where grandmother's here and aunty is here.

Nora's Top Destinations

* **Nairobi:** You have the mountains 40 minutes away from the city. You have Nairobi National Park with five of the six biggest animals in the world. You have the coast, which is the Indian Ocean. It's mind-boggling!

* **Mombasa:** The Mombasa coast is a warm bath, crystal-clear sea. It's so beautiful. There's no rough waves, you can just go and swim. The food is a mix of Indian and African influences – you have pilau, biryani rice with meat dishes. The architecture is beautiful. You just don't hear about Mombasa, unless you have family from that region.

* **Dakar:** They have this corniche, this walkway that you walk on to view the sea. I like the fact that you can be in the city and still experience the coast. Even if you're not swimming, you can sit and relax.

Nora's Tips for Travel

* **Get educated:** Travelling is more of a learning process than any course I could take at college or university. I think most people learn by doing and by seeing and by involving your senses. I think for me, when it comes to travel, it's those experiential moments that stay with you.

* **Learn the language:** When I first went to Senegal, I really struggled to communicate. It's quite arrogant to think that they have to speak English. I learned Wolof, the local language. My French was barely there. But the second time, I had a bit more French. Most people speak French or Wolof. When you travel, you do have to think, am I prepared to learn and be okay with not being able to communicate in the same way as if I went to a place that speaks the same language as me? The interactions that you have are well worth it. That being said, people will try to communicate in so many ways, including body language, and are incredibly kind and patient.

* **Record your memories:** I wish I'd written more and taken more pictures. When I was travelling with my mother in Malaysia, I wanted her to be comfortable. It was so nice when we got a hotel upgrade because it was at the end of Eid. They call it Hari Raya in Malaysia. Moments like that I could forget about if she didn't remind me.

  I went to Cuba with a friend of mine ten years ago. Our hotel receptionist's grandmother taught us salsa in her apartment opposite the hotel. I remembered we had ten minutes with her. And then after that, what happened? I can't remember!

* **Plan versus going with the flow:** I've got to know where I'm sleeping and how I'm getting from A to B. If you arrive at night, think about how you are going to get from A to B, and make sure you know

which airport you are going to. There can be multiple airports in one city. If you haven't been to the country, do research. Do I know somebody who can help? Will transportation require a pricey cab?

* **Don't overplan once you are there:** Being present and enjoying the moment can be the source of your best memories.

* **Avoid being on your phone too much:** it is easy to do when travelling solo but remember to look up, listen, watch and learn. Otherwise you will miss out. Freeing your senses is how you can enjoy being somewhere new.

* **Safety:** I get the question, 'aren't you scared?' I'm quite a curious person. I like to learn about new places, but I also like to return to places that I've enjoyed. If I'm going to a hotel that doesn't have security, I avoid giving away too much information. If you sense that this person or situation is uncomfortable, go with your gut. I don't feel travel is particularly brave. I just feel like it's something that I enjoy doing. I use street smarts. Don't do things that you wouldn't normally feel comfortable with, especially if you're travelling alone.

***

Travelling can be powerful way to figure out who you are and learn more about yourself through interacting with environments that help you deepen and discover your history. It can also complicate the identity search and struggle. The key is to be aware of the mixed feelings this kind of travel can bring up. Keep your expectations easy. You don't need to solve a lifetime of identity questions in one trip! Take it slowly, and enjoy the ride and unfolding.

4
Inspiration
Choosing Home

Inspiration
Choosing Home

Augustine once said, 'Solvitur ambulando': it is solved by walking. Muhammad Asad wrote, 'If water stands motionless in a pool it grows stale and muddy but when it moves and flows it becomes clear: so, too, man in his wanderings.' Sometimes when I have a knotty thought or am trying to crystallise something for myself, movement helps. I am rebooting the machinery in my mind as the IT folks always instruct you when your computer is down. It is infuriating but somehow it seems to work. Shifts in scene create shifts in perspective. And sometimes, these are generative and inspirational. Sometimes it starts with being stuck and the process of moving helps you somehow become unstuck. Even when the destination or end is not certain, the journey and the detours can inspire us in creativity, work, friendships, or life paths that we never would have thought possible.

Inspiration

Aisha al-Adawiya is one of the most inspirational women I have had the privilege to speak to. She was born in 1944 and grew up in Alabama, in the racially segregated American south. After graduating high school in the early 1960s, she moved to New York with a dream to pursue a career as a singer. This move was transformative and her life would take a route she never expected. After hearing a lecture by civil and human rights leader Malcolm X, she converted to Islam. She met her late husband of 37 years in New York and became a prominent racial justice and women's rights advocate. Here are Aisha's words on following your bliss in travel.

That was a transformative time, the 1960s. Tell me about your early journey from Alabama to New York.

I came to New York from Alabama after I had graduated high school. I went to Brooklyn, New York, to live with a maternal aunt. I stayed with her very briefly and then moved to Greenwich Village. I wanted to pursue a singing career. Now I'm in Harlem.

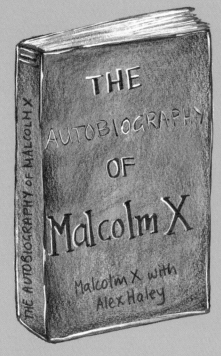

I wanted to leave my hometown as a young girl, and my parents saw that need in me very early on.

After I graduated high school, they allowed me to leave to come to New York but to live with family members. My dream was to pursue a singing career. The early '60s was a time of upheaval and a lot of change and transformation for young people here in the United States, looking for new ways of living, new modes of spirituality and searching to find oneself. That was the inspiration that kept me searching for something, spiritual guidelines to live my life by, and Islam found me.

I began to study Islam and find teachers that could mentor me about the religion and also, based on some of the early teachings of Malcolm X, to get a deeper understanding of who I was as a young Black woman in the United States, as an African in the Americas. That continues to be transformative for me and countless others. I was certainly ready to make additional changes in my life because I found that the environment at the time, although it was a heady time, it was a really strong learning environment on so many levels.

I was searching for spiritual guidance. Alhamdulillah, Islam was that thing that saved me from myself, quite literally. As young people coming into the sixties and into Greenwich Village of all places – I don't know if you are familiar with it, Greenwich Village, but it was the place to be, you know – there were a lot of great things that were happening at the time but there were also trends that could be destructive if you were not rightly guided. That's been the journey that I've been on since. I continue to try and travel that road. It's been a beautiful journey.

ha al-Adawiya

Inspiration

Can you describe listening to Malcolm X speak?

I was just captivated by the social critique that Malcolm did of injustice in the United States and internationally and how we as African Americans figured into that equation. That continues to be a learning experience for me. Nowadays, we're going back and listening to those speeches and those talks by Malcolm. All these years later, they resonate like he's talking today, because the challenges, the injustices, they remain, sometimes more palpable than ever. I didn't know Malcolm personally. I became friends with his wife Betty later.

We were friends until she passed away. But Malcolm Malik Shabazz is still my mentor. The message really resonated then and it continues to resonate very deeply and strongly, very powerfully every day.

Were your parents shocked by your conversion?

I was blessed. I do know people who embraced Islam, and after they did, their parents quite literally disowned them and many were thrown out of their homes for adopting this new religion, this strange religion, for them, as most of our families were Christian. But my family was very beautiful. They were very open. They trusted me and they allowed me to grow and flourish in my own way. I'm very thankful for that to this very day. They never objected to anything.

I was a shy girl, coming from the south, just searching for something to guide my life by. I think as a great-grandmother, I think what all parents want is to see that their children are happy and thriving. They could see that in me. My parents were great. The only thing my father asked me was, why did I change my name? Once he was satisfied with that, that was it. I'm thankful and grateful in so many ways for their trust in me and their ability to see me.

It was New York where all these ideas were, where all this creativity was, all these people were. So this journey was really life-transformative for you, wasn't it?

It was life-transforming. I came from the segregated south. I was already primed for resistance living in that environment, seeing the injustice that was perpetrated against Black people in my town. I was aware, living in a small town, the Black community was like an extended family. My experience was that I was very protected from a lot of things and began to realise and experience the harms, the real harms as I grew up and moved out into the world.

I was already on a journey because I was having experiences early on in my town as a young girl living in that environment where it's not acceptable to do things like speak back to white people. I always found myself speaking back which was not okay. It could be dangerous. It could be downright life-threatening. In retrospect, I think about my parents, the concern that they must have had for their children and how to protect them. I already grew up in an environment where I was no stranger to racism and bigotry at a very early age. I was looking for a way to resist all my life, quite frankly.

Inspiration

What inspired you to travel to New York from Alabama as a girl, when you've been trained and conditioned to feel like you can't assert yourself. So many women and many women of colour are often made to feel self-doubt in making bold choices.

I think it is not just women of colour. I think women find ourselves confined to boxes that are assigned to us. But my life was changing. I believe in Allah's qadr: what is willed for me will be there. I was already at a very early age seeking ways to address the issues that were impacting my life and my society and my community. As I grew older and became exposed to people, other people who were travelling the same path, I began to mature and find alliances. You find powerful mentors. We don't do these things on our own. You know that there are shoulders that we stand on and we are coming from communities where storytelling and the community feed you the information that you need for survival.

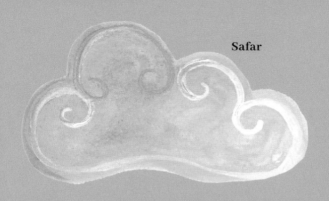

Aisha's Guide to Inspiring Travel

* Don't be afraid to challenge the status quo and to live life fully. Do not be selfish and certainly not arrogant.

* You catch more flies with honey than you do with vinegar.

* If you give a smile to a person, usually you'll get one back.

* Be open to the world and to the possibilities.

* Value who you are.

Inspiration

Your life experience gave you a finely attuned antenna to injustice. How did travel sharpen your politics?

As you grow older and are exposed to different communities, you begin to see that many of the issues that are impacting you at home are impacting other people as well. I also found myself eager to be with other people who were struggling for liberation. I consider that as 'home', to be in those communities with people who are conscious about the issues and who are willing and dare to see them, to address them and to resist them.

New York is like many countries in one city. It is like the U.N. Even before I began to travel outside of the United States, I could already experience that right here in New York. People coming from every place. I always sought those environments where I was in relationship with people from all over the world and so I could relate to them. I could see the commonality that we had on so many issues, not just issues of oppression and abuse, but beautiful things as well. I have travelled to Pakistan, Egypt, Saudi Arabia, Morocco, Geneva, Benin, Niger, Mali, UAE and Turkey. I seek out these experiences, these environments where I can be in community with people from all over the world. Of course, we're seeking similar values, so that we can all grow together, prosper and thrive.

Did you find soulmates in that mix?

Well, I was married to a man from Pakistan for thirty-seven years!
He was Muslim. I was Muslim. We were going through the same
New York community to study, to worship. He was always one of
those young men who was there. I knew him for several years and
I had observed, this was a serious, lovely young man, part of the
community, and this was a life partner.

**What is your advice for young women who might be afraid of taking
that step? How do you get the courage to embrace your qadr?**

My husband used to say, 'Face the challenges boldly.' That's my
advice, not only to young women, but to everyone who's striving
to come into their own. Do not to be afraid. Arm yourself with
knowledge. Be clear about what your bottom line is: this is the most
important thing. You must have a sense of who you are and be
honest about that. Put yourself in an environment where that can
be nurtured and challenged to grow to new heights.

"Inspiration can be like a butterfly, hard to grasp if you reach for it, but sometimes it settles on you mystically when you least expect it."

Aisha's story of how she allowed the world to speak to her and change her and the power there is in changing your environment and humbly seeking to learn from others reminded me of the importance of listening and observing.

When I was in Japan in 2019, my favourite sight was watching Mt Fuji at Lake Kawaguchiko. I had accidently booked a week's stay in this quiet locale with a magnificent lake. There was not much to do. But I started to lean into just being still and watching the glorious snow-capped mountain volcano. Every day I watched the mountain in high visibility, under clouds, at sunset and early in the morning.

It reminded me that everything has a season in nature; and we too, as humans have our dawns and dusks; our moments in sun and times when there are clouds in our skies.

Inspiration

Like all great things in nature; Mt Fuji reminded me to be proud, unapologetic and know your power. It would be ridiculous for Fuji not to be Fuji or hide herself and shrink away or pretend to be the lake or sky. Fuji is not saying 'Sorry! Sorry for existing!' Fuji is saying, 'here I am in my majesty and beauty'. I have often felt, as a Muslim in the west this sense of tension at not ever really feeling like I belong. Being in Japan made me realise perhaps I have to be more Fuji-like. I am here to stay and this world, the country I was raised in, they also belong to me and I don't have to apologise or be fearful for existing.

Inspiration can be like a butterfly, hard to grasp if you reach for it, but sometimes it settles on you mystically when you least expect it. Aisha's story reminds me to be open to the journey, even if you don't know the end point, because it is the people and detours along the way that can be the most fertile inspirations for growth in our lives. Inspiration is going with the flow, and allowing the world to speak to us as we move through it. It is letting those chance encounters and synchronicities to work their magic in our lives and change us in ways we could never have dreamed of.

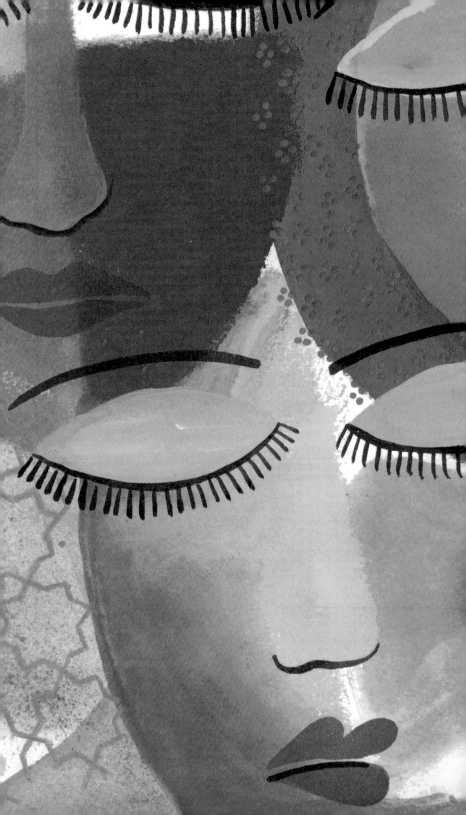

5
Confidence

Confidence

There's nothing that helps build confidence like being thrown out of your comfort zone and facing a challenging situation. I personally struggled with assertiveness and travel has allowed me to develop skills that make me confident in my ability to meet whatever life throws at me.

Confidence when travelling can be built from simple things, like problem-solving how to get from the airport to the hotel, exchanging currency, negotiating at the market or getting to a restaurant using maps. I realised that confidence is not innate but something you develop by challenging yourself and never is challenge and fear more pronounced than when you are trying to do basic things in a new environment.

In 2014 I lived in Amman for three months to study Arabic. The week I arrived in Amman, I gathered a crowd of students, eager for an outing to a local restaurant, to celebrate my 30th birthday with me over golden trays of mansaf and maqlooba. It occurred to me that in all the excitement of being in a new place, with strangers who had no idea about my past, straining my brain to learn new things, I had forgotten to be depressed about turning 30. It gave me the confidence to start shedding the stress load and, like a caterpillar, prepare for a new decade in my thirties.

Later, I remember trying to buy a pillow at Carrefour, the local supermarket but when I tried to tell the clerk what I needed, I forgot the word for pillow. I left embarrassed and without my pillow and cried in frustration. Days later, I regrouped. I practiced my Arabic to the point of confidence. I mustered the courage to ask again, and this time, I came home triumphant, pillow in hand, excited to get a good night's sleep. Taxis were a challenge, especially if you didn't negotiate before leaving or ask them to turn on the meter. Sometimes I was so wracked with nerves that I would sweat, worried that I would not be able to communicate or assert myself with confidence. Buying a pillow or taking a taxi by yourself might seem like a simple task

in your home city but simple things can seem very complicated in a new place. These moments gave me the reassurance that I could make my way and overcome my fears. What is initially stressful will soon become easier.

To be honest, though, it was a relief to occupy my mind with Arabic conjugations and pillows at that point in my life. I had just been made redundant at my dream journalism job and had to move back to my parents' home in Sydney after a decade of travelling and living in city share houses. And I was about to turn 30.

My confidence was at a low point, and I struggled to think of what was next for me.

The crisis also presented an opportunity. I had always wanted to learn Arabic, both for work and to connect with my faith. I decided to see how far I could take my meagre savings and I became a student again. I rediscovered my love for language and for getting to know new people — one of the reasons I became a journalist in the first place.

Confidence

For Raidah, a Malay-Australian writer and mum of three, sharpening and developing her intuition while travelling also boosted her confidence. She gained the courage to learn and say what she liked and disliked, a privilege she never felt she had before, especially as an autistic woman. Raidah said that as a neurodiverse child, she often come up against messages to not be disruptive, to sit still, to listen and to follow the rules. She felt this at times enforced a passivity and obedience to authority she didn't want for her daughters. 'That's something I want to teach my children, especially my daughters: to listen to their intuition.'

Travelling to Jordan as an Arabic student like me, and later to Hajj helped Raidah develop a sense of confidence in herself and her abilities and judgement, something she never had before. When you are travelling, you have to make big decisions fast, and be clear and emphatic to get your message across in a place where there is often no patience for indecisiveness. In a busy crowd, in a queue, in a taxi, or at the station, people do not have time for you to be confused about what you want and where you are going.

'It made me realise: I have agency. I have the ability to stand up for myself. I have the ability to leave if someone is not healthy. I have the ability to choose the type of people I want to hang out with.'

For Raidah, this meant sometimes breaking off from the 'cool' single travellers with whom she struggled to match social cues and find her own niche. This niche was usually mothers with young babies whom she adored spending time with.

When I first went to Paris at 25, going to the iconic Louvre art museum felt like one of the 'must-do' things, even though I hated museums and felt claustrophobic in them. I remember I stared at the line outside the art museum which was about 1 kilometre (0.6 mile) long. I then thought guiltily of instead heading to a café to eat cheese and croissants. As I weighed my options, cheese and croissants won out every time. This obligation to cross things off a checklist was an inherited social standard like being obliging or feeling that there was a right way to do things even if you really didn't feel like it. Letting go of those expectations and going with the flow was hard to do, but I enjoyed myself so much more when I followed my fancy, even if it just meant people-watching, eating in cafés, and walking the city.

For Farah, the key to enjoying travel was to take the good with the bad and let go of comparisons and expectations that travel had to look like a postcard or Instagram story of a stylised getaway. Most of the things involved in travel – carrying bags and getting lost in the sweaty heat – are not perfect Insta moments. Farah says it was important not to romanticise travel, understanding it comes with all the hazards of life anywhere. 'It's like most experiences of life. Sometimes they are just one thing after another. You lose your passport. Your bags get lost. You sit next to somebody who is irritating you. This is just the nature of human interactions and relationships.'

Farah says sometimes the awful moments of getting lost or ripped off or simply deciding you're not compatible with your travel buddy are all learning experiences. They teach you to be patient, to be savvy, to plan for things not always going your way. 'There are always going to be things you don't understand. But how great is it that you get to do it in some place that's completely different from where you were yesterday?'

Travelling Solo

The idea of solo travel can be daunting. But there are things about it that definitely have their perks: you can travel at your own pace, you are not hampered by someone else's preferences and schedules and you can wake up whenever you like. As someone who likes a sleep-in, this is my favourite part of solo travel!

Solo travellers are also more likely to meet new people. It can be a confidence-building tool and a way to learn about yourself (as well as perfect your selfie game).

'I didn't really get to do a lot of solo travel before I got married or had kids,' Academic and writer Dr Susan Carland tells me. 'My first solo trip was in my late twenties. It was the first time that I left both my kids to travel alone. It would be even longer, perhaps fifteen years ago and I was 25. I was going for a conference in Spain. (Husband) Waleed and the kids stayed at home by themselves.

Confidence

I was nervous because I hadn't travelled by myself as a woman. I didn't know what was going to happen. It was so good for my confidence that I just had to work out how to take a bus by myself in a country where they don't speak English and hope for the best. I had to be confident enough to sit in a restaurant by myself and have dinner. I came away feeling proud of myself that I did it. I did those things by myself as a single woman in a hijab. I felt so empowered – it's such a cliché word, but I felt good about myself.'

Getting sick in an unfamiliar place can be daunting, especially with no family around you. Margari Aziza-Hill, an American writer and academic who I speak to later on, fell ill several times on her first time overseas. But being sick deepened her faith and her confidence in her own abilities to look after herself: 'I felt closer to God being in those isolated moments where I had nothing else. You know nobody here and you have to figure it out. I came back with a richer experience. Travelling can be hard, but some of those hardships in travel brought me closer to Allah.'

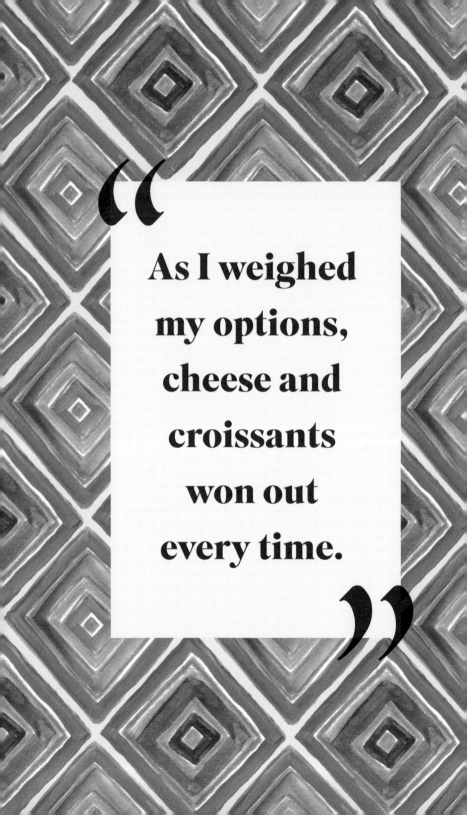

"As I weighed my options, cheese and croissants won out every time."

I also spoke to engineer and author **Yassmin Abdel-Magied** about her experiences and tips for solo travel. Her conversation with me is set out below.

What do you love most about solo travel?

I like travelling by myself because I like the headspace that it gives me. I think that my life, alhamdulillah, it's very full. I am constantly on the move and constantly doing things. But it doesn't leave a lot of space for my mind to rest. You need that for creativity, for original thought, to kind of recoup. I've always really valued the times where I get to be on a plane. When you head off to the airport and you know that you're going to be on your own for maybe 25 hours before you actually have to sit down and have another conversation with another person, a proper one. That's your own time. You don't owe anyone anything. It's the journey of moving forward, literally, whether you're on a train or on a plane. The primary joy of solo travel is that headspace and the freedom to go where your curiosity takes you. You don't have to negotiate what it is that you want to do.

How is it travelling as a Muslim woman?

I'm very much driven by my curiosity and desires as I'm moving through a place. The challenge, of course, is that I am an African Muslim woman wearing a hijab. I don't always feel safe everywhere. I'm much more cautious. I'm much more likely to take the more expensive and cautious route in taking transport, even if I'm on a very tight budget, versus one where I expose myself to risk.

Do you take any other safety precautions?

On my first trip overseas by myself, I was going to, funnily enough, Paris, for a three-week engineering course. I was 18. It was my first trip. I was so stoked. I couldn't believe my parents let me go. My dad sat me down and he properly gave me the speech: 'You know, nothing is safe, don't even make eye contact with anyone!' I had a money belt. I had money in my shoe and head scarf. I was prepared! I remembered he said to me, 'Do you remember that film where that man had a daughter kidnapped?' He meant *Taken*, the Liam Neeson film. He's like, 'I don't have that man's resources. If you get kidnapped, you're on your own.' And I was like, 'okay!' [She laughs.]

How do you make friends?

I don't drink but friends might go to a bar by themselves. There are too many uncontrolled variables in that kind of environment for me.

When I went to Switzerland for the first time, there was a handful of people on the slopes, and they'd be like, 'Oh, you know, why don't you come out and hang out with us.' The idea was for me to join a bunch of strangers getting drunk and it will be really fun. I was like, no. It was one step too far. For me, the adventure was already being in that place and learning how to ski. One night I found a fancy restaurant that I could afford and went by myself. It was low-key and halal and that was the treat I gave myself because I didn't feel like I had the capacity or the desire to do maybe what other people might see as the 'fun' stuff. It was great!

If I make new friends while I'm travelling, it tends actually to be via the Internet. I might share on social media that I'm in a particular place, and somebody might reach out and say 'Go to this restaurant' or 'I'm here as well, maybe let's meet up.' I've actually found people that way when I'm travelling by myself, as opposed to organically in the environment.

Travelling
as a
Mother

Confidence

When Tasneem planned her first trip abroad to her parents' ancestral homelands of Kenya and Tanzania, she was in her forties with three grown-up children. But she still remembered feeling guilty. When she was questioned by others about 'leaving her kids', she often felt a sense of judgment. 'A man would not be asked that question!' she tells me. Often this question would be asked by others who could afford to travel with their whole families. The unspoken implication made her over-compensate in preparing her children. 'No one leaves their kids and walks out of the house! The amount of planning I did to take that trip, the number of lunches and dinners I prepared and froze, the organisation I did, including creating school pick-up and after-pick-up timetables!' Tasneem laughs incredulously.

Of course no children were harmed in this anecdote. I can't think of a better role model than a mother who pursues her own needs and dreams. Tasneem's first trip was life-changing, igniting a decade-long love of travel.

***

Dr Susan Carland offers a perspective from the other end of the spectrum. Nearly two decades ago, newly married and finding herself a mum-to-be in her twenties, Susan and her husband Waleed Aly decided to forge ahead with a planned trip with a baby in tow. Susan discovered a way of experiencing the world she never would have thought possible. Here I chat to Susan about travelling with a baby, and other travel adventures and tips.

What are your memorable travel experiences?

I've done a lot of travel, which has been nice, and I feel very lucky. A lot of it has been with my family because I got married and had a baby very young. I got married when I was 21 or 22. I had my eldest by the time I was 23. My husband and I had been planning a trip and we found out at the same time I was pregnant.

We thought, we'll just do the trip with the baby. Like, how hard can it be? We thought, let's do this! Like idiots! We put our baby in a backpack and we went to Egypt, Spain, and Italy with the baby and it was amazing. It was just the best six weeks. That was a life-changing trip because so many people were like, 'Oh, no, travelling with a baby is terrible. It's going to be awful and stressful,' and it was fantastic! We still talk about it as one of the best trips we've ever done.

Dr Susan Carland

I think that was nice, because if it had been bad, or if we had convinced ourselves or had been convinced by others that you couldn't travel with kids, having had children so young, we just wouldn't have travelled at all. We were just determined that we can make this work. We have travelled so much with our children, both of them, from the time they were teeny tiny babies. Otherwise we would have had to wait till we were 50.

It's amazing how you just thought, 'Hey, I'm going to do this!'

We didn't have much money but it was such a wonderful trip. We travelled with the baby to countries which are very family orientated. We were treated so special by people. We would be eating in a restaurant in Spain and the baby would be fussing and here you would probably get dirty looks. But they were trying to give the baby lollies and really being super nice. We went to this museum in Italy and there was just this ridiculous queue and the security guard saw us and saw we had the baby in a backpack. They were like: 'This way!' They took us to the front and through this secret entrance. People were being so nice about having a baby, like it was an asset.

I remember our daughter having her first ice cream gelato when we were in the Vatican. She was covered in chocolate ice cream, chasing after pigeons, as happy as anything. It was just little moments like that we never would have had if we didn't have a baby with us. If she was with us, she was happy. When she slept, we put her in the pram or backpack, pushed her around and she slept on the bed with us.

You would have missed her if she wasn't there.

It would have been a totally different trip, and it would have been a great trip as well. But having her added such a lovely element and a way to connect with people and just proved to us this absolutely can be done. Don't listen to people who tell you that you can't. We did it and it was great. It was really good. You are exhausted when you have a baby whether you're sitting at home or not. I'm exhausted and sleep-deprived here at home in Melbourne. So I thought, why don't I be exhausted and sleep-deprived in Italy? We realised just how different — and not in a good way — some Western countries are in regards to kids. There is this separation, in that children don't belong, or they are not welcome in the same way. It's a pity, I think.

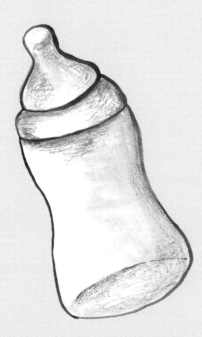

Have you ever experienced Islamophobia abroad?

Some people made it very apparent when they didn't like having me, a hijabi Muslim, around. But even in the Spanish town of Santiago de Compostela where I was once staying, there would always be people who would go out of their way to be nice to me as well. I try to really pay attention to that, too.

I didn't let it make me sort of dismiss an entire town, because of course, there are always going to be some bigoted people. I didn't want to do that to myself and think, well, I can't leave my room, and everyone's so mean because there were these people that were horrible to me in a restaurant. There was also the waiter who was nice and the guy who ran the tiny hotel I was staying in: he went out of his way to be nice to me as well. I was conscious of trying to focus on that too. It would have been easy to say everyone is mean, I can't do this as a Muslim woman, they are hostile and horrible. There was a part of me that was also, 'Stuff you! I'm not going to let you ruin my trip.' I did the things I wanted to do and I went to see the things I wanted to see. I felt that it was important. I didn't want that to be the last word on the trip.

Your identity is so complex, how has travel deepened or made you think about identity?

Identity can be complex, especially as a white woman who wears the hijab. There are a lot of parts of the Muslim world that cannot compute that. They cannot understand how you can be a Muslim who is white. They would assume that I was wearing the hijab as a costume! I'm like, why would I do that? It was obvious that I wasn't. Sometimes, for example, you're travelling in a Muslim country or a place with a big mosque and there will be tours going in. You can tell the white women who put on a little scarf to be respectful. I don't look like that! I wear a hijab the way a Muslim does. I cover all my hair. I remember going to a mosque in Malaysia. I was in a hijab and abaya which is a long dress. I wanted to pray. The guys at the door were like, 'No, only Islam.' I'm like, 'I'm Muslim!' They couldn't compute it. For them, in this culture, your religion is Muslim, and in that culture, it is Christian and there is no bleed-over.

Also I feel like in Australia so often I'm seen as not making sense. How can you be Muslim and a white Australian? The first time I went to a Muslim-majority country, I thought finally I will belong. They were just as confused and not wanting to let me into the mosque. Similar things have happened in other countries I've been to, where I have to retake my shahada in front of them, and in some places, I have had to recite suras of the Quran to convince them to let me in, and that I am, in fact, Muslim. I'm not a tourist! I'm not a spy! I just want to come to pray!

Were there any spiritually enriching experiences?

I think I certainly had those moments of spiritual peace when I was in Granada, Spain. The Alhambra is just astounding and probably my favourite place on Earth. But there is also a mosque that's opposite the Alhambra that I went into when I was travelling there by myself. I spent ages, just being there. It was such a peaceful space. I think probably the other time I felt that was doing Umra, going to the Prophet's Mosque and then going to the Kaaba in Saudi – I've done that twice in the last few years. I was warned so much before I went, 'you'll probably get sexually harassed', or 'the guards are so sexist.' But even with that, the peace I felt there, the serenity, for someone who, like I said, doesn't really belong anywhere: I felt like I belonged there. I think because my sense of belonging wasn't pegged to the people around me telling me if I belong. It's the certainty of knowing I belong to this faith, this faith that I chose. I've been Muslim now for longer than I haven't. I chose this faith. Maybe I don't belong in a place but I belong in this religion and these two places are the religion. They are so crucial to the faith that I feel like I belong here. Everything sort of makes sense here. Even though these people around me are from a million different cultural backgrounds, we can't talk to each other, we all look different, the security guard is telling me I shouldn't be praying here as a woman – even with all that, it's like being in the eye of the storm. I'd go back every month if I could.

Confidence

When you are travelling as a westerner how do you deal with your passport privilege and also travelling sustainably?

You just have to acknowledge your outrageous privilege. None of us deserve the privilege of our cultural background, our race, our ability level. All we can do is say, 'Well, what do I do with this privilege that I don't deserve?' So, when we travel, what can we do with it? How can we try to be the kind of tourist that leaves as little negative impact on the place as possible and does as much as possible to support the local economy? It is by not being a jerk to the people there, from the way you tip to the way you take photos, all the way to how you move through a space, and the way you listen to people who talk and by observing cultural norms. Yes, we are privileged but I don't think we should never travel because we must get to know the world. The alternative is otherwise that we stay in our privileged bubble. I don't think that's right, either. Travel as humbly as possible and just try to be respectful visitors in the place.

***

Confidence comes with stretching your muscles to deal with unfamiliar and sometimes stressful situations. Whether it is travelling solo, travelling as a mum or even getting sick, sometimes the unconventional and unexpected experiences can be the most confidence building. Remember, there is no 'one' way to travel and there is no perfect path or guarantee all will go smoothly. So go easy on yourself. Sometimes journeying means figuring it out as you go along and making mistakes along the way.

Susan's Top Tips for Travel

* **Go for it.** If you can, travel as much as you can. It's good for your mind and it's good for your soul. It's good for your empathy.

* **Go with others.** If you're feeling nervous, that is okay. I don't think I would ever dismiss someone who says they are nervous about travelling to certain places, because I think often, we're reading that right. That's a very clear-eyed assessment of the reality of being a woman in the world. Could you travel with a couple of other girlfriends? Do you have a family member you get on really well with, or a sibling? Go in a group to start. Go with people that you feel comfortable with.

* **Google.** If you're travelling by yourself, do a lot of research beforehand about places to stay. There are a lot of really good reviews by single women who could have stayed there before. Send the advice down the line to other women about good places to stay that you felt safe, including good restaurants, etc. Share that information with people and other women digitally.

* **Build your confidence up.** If you're feeling nervous, and it's your first trip, start easy. Why don't you go interstate with a girlfriend, or by yourself, and see how that goes, having to manage flights and accommodation?

Susan's Advice on Dealing with Hairy Travel Situations

When you travel, bad things will happen. Hopefully you won't get attacked or anything like that but your luggage might go missing, you'll get charged $10 for a glass of milk at the hotel, you'll miss the train or someone will convince you to buy a rug you didn't want. It will be frustrating and upsetting. But the good thing about travel is those terrible things that happen always make the best stories. Like when you suddenly realise, this swindler put us on the wrong train and now we have travelled eight hours in the Sri Lankan countryside and we don't know where we are! This is a nightmare. I promise you, those moments make the best stories. As long as there's nothing truly awful, they will be the things that you laugh about and reflect on the most when you come back. The beautiful things are good and lovely, but weirdly it's the bad stuff you will remember most fondly!

6

The Politics
of Travel

The Politics of Travel

You can't talk about travel and journeying without talking about privilege. Passport privilege. Financial privilege. The politics of being a tourist. Who gets to travel and how? Can you travel in a decolonial and sustainable way? What about travelling on a budget? How do you avoid perpetuating or replicating problematic dynamics?

***

Margari Aziza-Hill is deeply conscious of the politics of privilege. Margari is the co-founder and executive director of the Muslim Anti-Racism collaborative. She has been published in 'How to fight White Supremacy' (2018) among other publications. Her research includes anti-colonial resistance among West Africans in Sudan during the 20th century and the criminalisation of Black Muslims.

Margari Aziza-Hill

Safar

Margari was born in New Jersey and grew up in San Jose, in northern California. She embraced Islam at 19 years old in 1994. Margari had a wanderlust for travel but no way to actualise her dream. Once an Islamic teacher told her that to really understand the Quran, you needed to learn Arabic and for that you needed to study abroad. At the time Margari was a broke teenager: 'I asked him, how does someone like me do that? I don't have any money. I'm broke. I'm a woman. How can someone like me learn? I was so passionate about travel, I wanted to learn and it just seemed like this impossible thing.'

Margari loved writing historical fiction and often had her stories set in ancient Andalusia and Morocco. 'I actually gave up writing because I thought I'll never be able to go there. It was dramatic!' Margari's dream became a reality when she was accepted into graduate school: Stanford university on a scholarship. It was a dream-come-true for a working-class girl from Jersey. The prestigious program offered a grant to travel abroad as part of a foreign language course: Morocco. Margari couldn't believe it.

'Being a student and all of a sudden, I'm in this place I dreamed about, that I wrote about. I just thought it was so impossible. Like how does someone like me go abroad? My affluent friends went to Hajj and abroad. It was a different time. People because of their networks were invited to different things but I didn't have the same opportunity to book a flight, get shots, figure out how to get a passport and insurance. Travel was something other people did! So for me, getting into an elite graduate program and educational opportunities opened up everything that was closed to me.'

The Politics of Travel

Forging a path in the academy was not easy. Margari's student colleagues were middle-class white American students, many of whom had travelled extensively. It was Margari's first journey abroad. She was in her late twenties, recently divorced, newly independent, and she was nervous and overwhelmed. It didn't help that Margari's first flight experience was anything but smooth. She was flying from California to Morocco with stopovers in New York and France. A thunderstorm meant the plane had to circle endlessly before landing in New York, forcing her to find another connecting flight to France. A missed connection meant an already nervous Margari had to spend the night in the airport. When she finally landed in Fez and was met by two student leaders, she tried nervously to practice her basic formal Arabic.

But overall it was a soft landing. Margari and her fellow students explored the country in guided tour vans. In the six weeks Margari was in Morocco, she visited numerous locations including Marrakesh and Tafilalt, one of the largest oasis regions in Morocco. 'For me this was an absolute dream.'

Safar

A visit to the Zawiya Tijani, a complex commemorating the 18th-century Sufi leader Ahmed Tijani, changed her life and shaped her research for years to come. 'There were these women pilgrims from West Africa, from Senegal and Mali, you could see the different types of clothes they wore and the openness and fluidity around the hijab, as well as Moroccan women with the traditional jellabiya. For me the experience of praying side by side with women from West Africa and Morocco in this ziyarat was a profound experience of feeling like I am part of the umma.' The Tijani tariqa, their history of anti-racist scholarship and ziyarat became key research interests for Margari.

The trip also meant reconciling different kinds of privilege: 'It's not easy being one of the few Black Muslims in a program where most of the students have their own orientalism and bias coming out.' There were students who complained about street harassment in a way that made Margari's blood boil not because it didn't exist but because it was assumed to be unique to where they were. Margari's own experience growing up in American cities – being catcalled and harassed in East San Jose where she grew up, a phenomenon that fuelled programs like the 'Hollaback' anti-harassment campaign – made her aware of sexual harassment as a global problem. But she was also hyper-aware of it as a tourist, drawing questions as a young woman travelling alone.

'When you're travelling abroad you just see how rude Westerners can be,' Margari said. There were times Westerners expected her to move out of the way. There were Western men who would proposition her in restaurants, wondering why a Black woman would be eating alone at an expensive restaurant. 'You would see yourself as part of the props of the background. I became very sensitive to the power dynamics of tourists.' At times being able to 'blend in' worked to Margari's benefit. There were times tourists and locals were confused about her identity and she was able to walk into local cabs, markets and mosques without query. Other times it backfired, when it was assumed she would have the know-how of a local but was confused about how to use a bathroom water hose or her Arabic was misunderstood or her Western name and Islamic identity was questioned.

Travelling to Morocco made her aware of the deep history her newly acquired faith had in the lands of her ancestors: 'I had never been to the African continent. I'm African American and I'm also Muslim. There's this part intellectually where you read about your

ancestors but you know, for me it was mainly feeling like being on the fringes of Muslim communities in the US, when you're working-class, don't have a lot of money, single or have the stigma of being a divorcee.' But like her teacher had promised, the experience was life-changing: 'It definitely changed my life and my outlook and understanding around Islam, as more experientially informed and different from the types of ways I understood Islam as an American convert.' Margari says that seeing Moroccans who looked like her and being surrounded by Muslims felt 'amazing.' 'In the south of Morocco I saw people who looked not only like me but also my daughter and my family, who are mixed-race, with sandy curly hair and different shades of brown.'

The idea of privilege can be shape-shifting and slippery, exercised in one context and erased in another.

'Travelling abroad as a Western Muslim is being deeply aware of one's privilege,' Margari said. Travelling in Europe, Margari was made deeply aware of the power of her US passport. 'If I travel in Europe, I can be seen a certain way and suddenly you can reverse that. Do I become a loud American to assert my rights? We did flash my blue passport sometimes to assert ourselves and not be stepped over.'

Her first Moroccan travel experience emboldened Margari. She went on to live in Egypt, visiting Mount Sinai and St Catherine's Monastery and later Kuwait. For Margari, one of the most heartwarming experiences was in Alexandria, Egypt. After a day at the beach, she realised that her hair, treated with oil, had clay

caked into it. Margari was stressed: 'I couldn't wash it out of my hair!' Margari had brought with her an arsenal of hair care from the States but she was unable to sort her hair drama despite her best efforts. But she was pleasantly surprised to find an abundance of salons that catered to her hair type. Hair gels she needed were easily available in Egyptian shops. 'Similar to African American hair, North Africans have curly hair, so they were able to do my hair. My hair looked so nice! I was walking down the street thinking, my hair is whipped!'

'Travel deepened what I wanted out of life. It was really amazing being a world traveller and being able to say things and communicate with people in different ways. It definitely was a confidence-builder.'

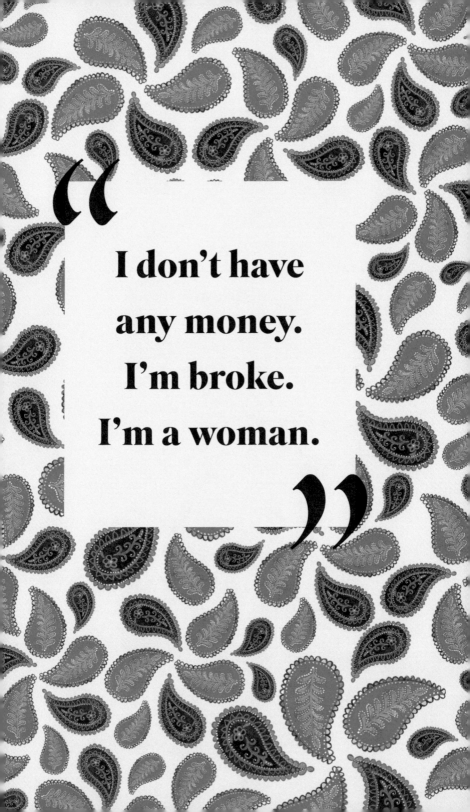

"I don't have any money. I'm broke. I'm a woman."

Margari's Tips for Travel

On a budget: There are things I didn't know coming from a working-class background. Sometimes you don't need a lot of money to travel. You can:

* Check out hostels.

* Consider taking up work while travelling, like teaching a language.

* Consider grants and sponsorship opportunities for travel, including educational opportunities or exchange programs.

* Link up with other female travellers who can share a network of support and shared resources and recommendations for flatmates and travel buddies.

* And don't forget to budget for tips. Nobody tells you how much you will have to spend in tips to almost everyone. But you have to budget it in, because you'll run out of money otherwise!

Flying while Muslim: 'I have to create a buffer time to deal with security as a Muslim!' says Margari. Like a lot of Muslim travellers, Margari has been detained at both Heathrow and US airports by security, with her passport flagged for visits to places considered 'hotspots.' Here she has a practical list for others who might face the same dilemmas she did while flying:

* Dress non-metal: 'I accept I'm going to be pulled over, so what am I wearing? Is it comfortable enough? Is it going to be able to withstand all the security, where they make you almost undress? I wear sweatpants, no wire in my bra, nothing metal on me, no pins in my hijab, and slip-on shoes. I try to keep it as simple as possible, so they can only stop you for buttons.'

* Don't be late! If you're rushing, it can be more difficult to get through security, especially if you are pulled over to a room.

* Bank in extra time for connector flights and for extra time in security.

* Declare any food, objects, or cash that need declaring.

Safar

When your identity has been so surveilled; and full of striving, like Margari, there is something so subversive and luxurious about embracing joy and pleasure and fun. For Margari this luxury was hard-won via grants and school opportunities. It can feel like repair to embrace the self-care of unplugging, to allow yourself a moment away from hustle and grind in a world where you are often told as a working class person or woman of colour that you have to be twice as good to get half as much.

In a canopy of stunning pink Sakura in Nara, Japan, my heart felt so happy surrounded by these ancient blooms. I felt able to let go of the need to be productive; of the striving and overachieving that I had sometimes let define my self-worth. I also felt a deep appreciation for the privilege of this experience, one that my parents would never have, as economic migrants to a new country. It was late March and my birthday in April was approaching.

The Japanese revere the Sakura – barren the whole year, they bloom during a brief window, the new shoots ushering in Spring. I waited patiently like all the locals. I made watching the spindly branches my only job. And finally by April we were suddenly flooded with Sakura. It's such a celebration, with every person's face in wonder and delight, taking photos and basking in the pink, red and white lining the country in colour. It's a national wonder.

What I loved was how underscoring the celebration is the bittersweetness of its temporality. Its very fragility and fleeting ephemerality make it more beautiful and precious because it will soon be gone. Underneath the joy is the deep lesson of acceptance, of the reality of the cycle of nature we are all bound by, which turns like clockwork through birth, death and regeneration. Every cherry blossom tree is different. Some old and gnarled, coiled, in open loops or wound tightly in straight buds, but they all bloom in in their own hour with their unique beauty. I too, could take my time.

***

Yassmin Abdel-Magied is one of the most thoughtful travellers I have met: an advocate for transformative justice and someone deeply interested in global solidarity movements who also has a deep sense of fun and curiosity. I thought she would be the perfect person to talk about how to both be aware of and leverage your privilege and also embrace and step boldly into a world that isn't always comfortable or safe for a young Black woman.

Tell me about your travel experiences.

The first time I travelled for pleasure was when I moved out of Australia to London in 2017. I didn't know anyone. I decided I needed a hobby and that hobby would be to learn to ski. I'd visited a place with snow once in my life, during summer. It wasn't even like I'd seen snow properly. I spent weeks Googling where to learn to ski. I spent all my savings paying for like a week in this ski resort in Switzerland called Zermatt. It just turns out that Zermatt is like one of the bougiest fancy ski resorts in the world. I didn't know this. The only place I could afford was this tiny attic, in some dodgy hotel. There was one other Black woman in the whole village and she sought me out.

Yassmin Abdel-Magied

Both of us were learning to ski. She was a 45-year-old woman with me in the baby section for skiiers. It was hilarious.

This also shows how unprepared I was. I wanted to practice French. I know that they speak French in Switzerland but Zermatt is in the German-speaking part of Switzerland. Nobody even wanted to speak to me in French so I pretty much spoke to no one for the week. One family I did speak to said that whenever they saw a Black person on the slopes, it was a sign of good luck. I was like, 'Am I a leprechaun? Like, am I a mythical creature?' [She laughs.]

Going there was like reverse colonialism!

That they made me pay very steeply for!

Tell me about your background.

My work meant I left Brisbane where I grew up and I moved to Perth when I was about 21 or 22 to work as a mechanical engineer on the oil rigs in Western Australia. When I was in Perth, it was an interruption to my life. I love trying out sports where I'm really not meant to be. I learned how to sail. I'd always joke to the sailing

people, 'Oh yeah, I'm just practising for my people-smuggling business,' which I thought was a hilarious joke – they did not. They had this rule where you weren't allowed to wear hats inside the club building and they were always like, 'Is that a hat?' about my hijab. 'Does that fit under the rules?' Because if you wear a hat, you had to buy everyone a bottle of alcohol. None of these rules were clearly set out for me.

Is it about disrupting space?

I will not deny there is a certain thrill in being in a place where people do not expect to see you. The power is in my hands. I'm not forced to be there. I'm choosing to be there so I can kind of play with their expectations, in a way, set the tone for the interactions. I find that thrilling and there's something quite exhilarating about it. There's this kind of weird undertone of 'this isn't a place you are meant to be.' By being there, by turning up, you are going against everyone's grain but nobody's going to say that to you. I just love walking that fine line.

How do you deal with this question of 'where are you from?' or identity in travelling?

It's very different to be asked where I'm from in Paris and London than when I live in Australia because my sense of self is not tied to that place. In a sense, I think it's very different to be asked where you're from in your own country. I've grown up in Brisbane all my life. Being asked where I'm from there erodes my sense of belonging in that environment, whereas in any other context, I can understand it because I don't speak the language. I perhaps have a bit more bandwidth to accept that question in a way that doesn't affect my sense of self which I appreciate is a real privilege of being able to choose where I want to be. I think the more I've moved, the less I even know the answer to the question of where I'm from.

How do you deal with the tension of navigating the privilege of travel as a tourist and also knowing the experiences of immigrants who experience exclusion?

It comes with completely different connotations, expectations, power dynamics and desires. I revel in being a traveller because that to me is where I can maintain a sense of power and agency. I was in Paris for a writer's residency so it wasn't like I sought Paris as a place to visit or a place to live. Spending time in a ski resort versus ending up living in Paris and trying to make a life there and having to constantly put myself in an environment where I feel that sense of unbelonging

or of being an outsider is vastly different. When I am trying to create a life there and I'm trying to be part of the society, it makes all the difference to how I feel.

How do you navigate your sense of social justice when you are travelling?

There is a James Baldwin quote: 'You think that you've experienced the most pain and then you read.' You think that your history is unique and then you travel, and you realise across the world in lots of different forms, there are lots of different stories of oppression and revolution and resilience and strength and wonder and beauty. There's something wondrous in that. It allows me to feel that there is space to build a global solidarity.

Safar

One of the groups that I've connected to are the Myanmar folks in the diaspora and I tried to help as much as possible with the Sudanese revolution. Even though our fights and our struggles are so different, I think the more I travel, the more I realise that there's more space for us to learn from each other. Of course, in relation to Sudan, my context was going to be different. My approach was going to be different. It was a real strong reminder, it's okay for me to have this relationship with my faith and with how I think it needs to operate in the world, as well as acknowledging that that is just not going to work in every context because, even though we might be born in the same place, our lived experiences are so different and therefore the conclusions that we come to are going to be radically different. I think the experience perhaps taught me how to be able to hold various truths simultaneously.

Tell me the story of being called to Monaco last-minute as a reporter for Formula One, trying desperately to find accommodation but only finding hotels for 500 Euro per night.

I'm literally parked outside mansions on the south of France, sleeping in my car! I wake up at five o'clock in the morning because I was freezing. I need to go to work in a few hours. I need to turn up to the F1 track, ready to impress and to do my job and interview people. And I'm filthy! I haven't had a shower in days. I also didn't speak French at the time. I needed to find somewhere I can shower. I didn't have internet on my phone so I couldn't look anything up. The only thing I knew was the word douche, French for shower. I walked into a random establishment asking for douche.

After about two hours of walking up and down the street being completely unsuccessful, I go into this bakery and see a Muslim woman behind the counter. I asked, 'Do you speak Arabic?' And she was like, 'Yeah.' I was like, 'Thank God.' I asked, 'Do you have anywhere where I can have a shower?' She was like, 'No, I don't.'

But then it just so happened that the person behind me in the line was an older lady who understood the conversation. She asked the bakery lady in French: 'Does this woman need a shower?' I was translated for by the shop owner. This woman says to me: 'My house is just around the corner. You can come in and have a shower if you want.'

I was ecstatic. I don't speak French. She doesn't speak English. She takes me to her place. It is 3 metres by 4 metres (10 feet by 13 feet). Out of a drawer she pulls out nice bread and makes me toast. I am in this place where there are millionaires on every corner. The person that showed me generosity and kindness was this woman with so little. It is a memory that I will always treasure.

Can we travel in a decolonial way, with environmental sustainability?

We think of travel as a modern thing but people have travelled since the beginning of time. Whenever there has been a community, there's always been one or two people in that community that have been curious about what life outside their world is like. They were merchants who took goods with them and returned with others. Travel has been part of our stories for longer than perhaps we might think. I think of travel as my birthright. Allah has given us a world full of wondrous places and people. For me, it's making sure that we travel with a sense of curiosity and humility and that when we go to a new place, we understand that it is not our place to ever tell anyone how they should be, that we should always approach things with an open mind.

The Politics of Travel

It's very important wherever I am to try to understand that place and its history. How can I potentially raise awareness in my own circles about an injustice that's happened in a place that we might not have even thought about and how can we connect our struggles?

It hasn't been easy and possible for people to just fly across the world. 100 and 500 years ago the technology wasn't there. We have this incredible opportunity and it should be honoured and it should be treasured and respected. Nobody has more right to it than you.

Yassmin's Tips for Travel

I love clothes and fashion. I try to find local artisans that are trying to maintain their culture through textiles to support and buy from.

* **Read and research:** Find out what does it look like to support sovereignty and pay respect to First Nations peoples when you visit somewhere.

* **Carbon credits:** Leave a light footprint by purchasing carbon credits.

Rather than coming from a place of guilt, come from a place of curiosity and honouring. Travel has always been in our histories, but the kind of travel that we get to do and who gets to do that travel has changed.

* **Journey in your own backyard:** 'My family had very little spare money growing up. It was my father's priority that we would go back to Sudan every two years because that was vital to who we were as a family. We had to sacrifice to make that happen. Everyone can't do huge international trips. Many people live paycheck to paycheck. I encourage people to think about what does it look like to have a traveller's mindset in your own city, in your own country, in your own state? I grew up in Queensland, Australia, and there's still so much of that state that I would love to visit. There are still so many different First Nations groups I would love to meet and to learn from. Travel doesn't have to be on the other side of the world. I think you can have that traveller's mindset, an approach of curiosity and humility and hunger to learn and that can exist wherever you are.'

Yassmin's Travel Rituals

'As soon as I move somewhere, I find a coffee shop. There was this one coffee shop that I essentially went to religiously for a year in Paris called Le Peloton Cafe. I've always liked the interaction in cafes. I've lived alone for a lot of my life, and I've often wondered, if I went missing, how long would they take to discover me? What would it take for people to notice I was missing? If I ever went missing, it would be good to go to my local cafes because there will be the people to tell you how long it's been since I've been around!' And her favourite place? 'For me, the London Library is a gem, a place where I can sit and either read or work.'

***

Travelling in a way that recognises privilege is an important part of being a conscious traveller. This could involve researching and honouring the First Nations history of a place you are visiting by engaging in an educational class; or supporting First Nations-owned tour operators and local businesses. Use the opportunity to build solidarity, learning and understanding. The key thing is respect; both in our inter-personal behaviour and our financial interactions.

7
Spirituality
Travelling to God

Spirituality
Travelling to God

I remember doing Hajj as a thirteen-year-old with my parents. I was too young to really understand the spiritual significance of what I was doing but the crowds, the emotions and the feeling of being part of something much larger than yourself, felt like being part of a global moment. My parents and sister and I wore ihram, plain white pilgrimage garments representing the equality of believers in front of God intended to erase signifiers of class, gender, race, social status, nationality and go beyond any of the things that usually define us.

We flew from Karachi to Jeddah, Saudi Arabia, where we would then make our way to the holy city of Makkah, where millions of pilgrims from all over the world visit to do seven circulations of the Kaaba, a cube-like structure Muslims believe was constructed by Prophet Ibrahim and his son Isma'il. Nearby, pilgrims run seven times along a tiled area between the hills Safa and Marwa, retracing the steps of Hajar, the wife of Ibrahim. Hajar was left alone in the desert with her baby Isma'il and so called out to God for help. On the seventh run between the hills, water miraculously gushed from the earth at her feet, the beginning of the well of Zam Zam. Her struggle and faith is commemorated as an act of tawakkul, trust in God. It is something I still feel emotional and awed by. The fact that one woman's journey is commemorated throughout time in the rituals of Hajj by millions of Muslims every year for hundreds of years is incredible to me. As a Muslim feminist, it's something I feel so proud to have witnessed as a young person.

We would also go on to climb Mount Arafat where the Prophet delivered his last sermon and ceremoniously throw stones at a pillar representing the place the devil tempted Ibrahim. It is a physical ritual reflecting the challenge of eternal 'inner' jihad, the deeper journey of conquering your nafs, the lower and ever-tempting ego.

At the time I didn't know any of this spiritual history. I remember endless walking, with huge crowds pressing in on me at all times. I remember wondering at the people and the vastness of the skies, the deserts and the tents we pitched in the mountainous areas.

***

Raidah Shah Idil

Spirituality

Raidah's Hajj in 2010 with her brother was formative. Raidah now lives in Kuala Lumpur but grew up in Sydney, Australia. Raidah was single at the time and living out of home by herself in Jordan for the first time that year. She was enjoying the independence and stress that came with branching out on her own while navigating a different culture and trying to learn a new language. Her brother was also in the country at the same time and a rushed plan was made up. Why not also go to Hajj since they were so close to Saudi Arabia?

For Raidah, the trip created some apprehension. One, she was a student on a limited budget and would need to do Hajj backpacker-style, using budget accommodation. And two, she was neurodiverse. The new social cues, overwhelming sensory stimulus, crowds, packed schedules and last-minute changes of a Hajj trip were potential challenges for her as a woman with autism.

At the time, she was part of a spiritual community in Jordan that discouraged medication. Raidah says that one of the best decisions she made was to continue with her medication anyway: 'Part of me felt like, "Oh man I want to experience highs without meds." My psychiatrist was like, 'No you're going to be with millions of other

people. It's best to be safe.' It was a decision she was happy to have made. 'I guess I internalised ableism, that I could only experience heights without meds. And then I thought, no, I need to stay well and I'm really glad I stuck to my guns.'

Raidah felt awed walking into Medina, the cool oasis city to which the Prophet Muhammad and the persecuted Muslims of Makkah once fled. Wandering the streets of Medina helped her relate to the religious stories of her childhood: 'It felt like a different colour. It felt green and it felt like peace. Like I stepped into a different realm.'

Giving herself downtime, water breaks and quiet time helped her take in moments of wonder in the midst of the crowds. 'It was a balancing act. But to me the most relaxing thing about being at Hajj was just sitting down and looking at the Kaaba and reflecting on the fact that there's a whole unseen world that I can't see. That's where Allah shows up clearest to me in my life, in times when my limitations could have overwhelmed me but I kept going. Seeing Allah through the fractures I have within myself because I couldn't have done Hajj solely by myself. I am aware of where I fall short but I got through it with Allah's help and my brother's help.'

Raidah said she often felt like an outsider in hierarchical religious organisations. At Hajj, she felt for the first time a connection to the tradition in a way that moved her whole soul. I had felt the same way when I was a teen. I registered that Islam was bigger than the expressions of it that many of us are raised with.

For Raidah, travelling for Hajj cemented her relationship to faith as something deeply personal, experiential and also rooted in bigger questions of justice and equality: 'Religion is not just about other

Raidah's Tips for Travelling with Neurodiversity or Disability

* Make sure to take the right medication dosage in advance for the days required of travel, and back up if needed.

* Arrange telehealth appointments in advance for medical support back home.

* Find a doctor who can offer a prescription if needed in your place of travel.

* Use a website to get advance itineraries to limit surprises.

Raidah's Tips for Tour and Travel Operators

* Offer time for sensory breaks including downtime and quiet areas; offer easy access to bathrooms, and mobility assistance.

* Ask in advance if people are neurodivergent or differently abled and what their needs might be, including dietary accommodation; sufficient warning about schedule changes in light of specific transportation requirements; and general flexibility.

people but it's between me and Allah and the way I manifest it, the way I choose to practice Islam.'

For young Raidah the trip was transformational. 'I kept getting drawn to this search for the answer outside of me, when it's always been inside of me, you know? So that's when I was able to let go of the magic pill or silver bullet and realise it's more about me growing my capacity for discomfort and uncertainty and knowing that everything doesn't always have to make sense. I can't see a solution right now but Allah is with me and He will unfold it for me slowly. I didn't have to pack up and go to the desert to find peace. I could find it here within me, now.'

For Raidah, then a single woman, the experience cemented her commitment to teach her kids faith that centred social justice for the marginalised, the poor and those who felt like outsiders: 'We're in a situation where people have huge followings and they're so powerful and have all this money. They forget about the very people Islam came to liberate and empower: women, the vulnerable, people with disabilities.' Raidah says many able-bodied hetero-cis-normative people who fit a tidy box of acceptability found it difficult to empathise with unfamiliar experiences of marginalisation. For Raidah, Hajj provided a pathway to a renewed spirituality that was paired with social consciousness and pride in her perspective as a disabled woman with a disabled child.

'I want to leave a legacy, with better systems in place for everyone. That's the prophetic way, to not just care about yourself and your immediate family, but by making change, as well as bringing awareness and accountability.'

For both me and Raidah, Hajj was a spiritual travel experience that was a reminder of both the collective and the individual and how we intersect. In the sea of people from around the world, it was comforting to know the collective was bigger, more vast and more diverse, than any one person or group. It transcended our personal disappointments and limitations. And within that collective, each traveller was making their own arduous individual physical and spiritual journey in the most public arena of the world but rooted deep within their soul and their own relationship with God.

Nature

Under the Stars

One of the most incredible spiritual experiences of my life was visiting Wadi Rum, a desert valley in Jordan, hosted by Bedouin Arabs for whom it was home. I felt overwhelmed and awed by such vastness. My modern brain was trained to do things a million miles an hour, busy with constant lists and meetings and distractions. Back home, life sometimes felt like a simulation mediated through the Internet. I had to retrain my brain to operate in this environment. I felt in the desert a sense of stillness and quietness I had not been able to access before.

Our guides navigated the terrain by the sun and by the stars. Tender spiced meat was prepared with coal fire under the ground, warm scents mingling with the cool evening desert air. I learned I had a poor sense of direction and zero survival skills and would have been lost or eaten by a predator in minutes if left to my own devices. It reaffirmed for me that our senses and skills can be sharpened if we cultivate and hone them.

The Bedouin's awareness of their physical environment was part of understanding they were interconnected with it and depended on it for their survival. In the city I was often in my head, divorced from my environment. I learned that sometimes, journeying is about staying still, quiet, listening, taking in the world around you and allowing it to speak to you.

Close to Home and the Sea

Travelling to the coast should take no more than an hour or two from anywhere in Sydney. Whenever I was overwhelmed or stressed, I got in my car and drove to the coast. Usually I would land in Sydney's iconic Coogee Beach, where would I sit at the promenade steps with a coffee and soaked in the ocean, observing its changing moods and colours as the waves hit the shore and the sun dances on the surface.

Spirituality

During COVID lockdowns, 5-kilometre (3-mile) limits were imposed, prohibiting travel across the city. When the imposition was lifted, I exhaled. Being kept from the coast under lockdown made me appreciate how lucky I was to live in a coastal city and visit what feels like a holiday destination in my own backyard. I watched the surfers and let my eyes linger on the horizon until the sun sets. I watched people walking the promenade or reclining on the sand and grass. I watched the young children clutching ice cream. When I am near the ocean, my mood instantly changes and I feel refreshed and energised.

Lockdowns made me appreciate how much travelling to places of natural beauty helped me connect to myself, how spiritually grounding and meditative it was. It made me realise how my excitement to travel overseas gave me an energy that I could re-create and channel in my own city.

Where do you go that makes you feel peaceful? Is it a park? A square? A mosque? An incredible sunset near a river, or sitting under your favourite tree? How can you de-familiarise the familiar and make a journey close to home something to marvel at?

Uluṟu

In 2015 my two sisters and I travelled to Uluṟu in Australia's Northern Territory, located in the red desert centre of the country. The site is 348 metres (1142 feet) high and has a circumference of 9.5 kilometres (6 miles). The sandstone cliff-faces and waterfalls are estimated to be about half a billion years old. The rock site is sacred to the Traditional Owners of the land, the Anangu people. Before the official 2019 ban, the Anangu welcomed tourists to visit and see Uluṟu but pled with tourists to not climb the rock, citing safety fears for the climbers. Over thirty-seven people had lost their lives attempting it since the 1950s. Many climbers had also littered the site with faeces and rubbish, polluting the clear streams that travel through the rsacred site.

As a traveller I felt immediately awed by the abundant free-flowing waterfalls and rock art painted in the caves. It felt like being close to a living, breathing home of knowledge. Cliffs as tall as buildings lay across the red expanse. I felt a sense of stillness and quiet. I was enveloped in the generosity and spirituality of the place. I didn't understand why anyone would even want to climb. Just being here was enough.

My sisters and I felt connected in a different way. We took the car out into the desert and talked for hours. In the midst of this vastness, we did not feel the need to rush. We had all the time in the world to just be. We have degraded so many of our environments, causing climate change, rising temperatures, floods and fires. I felt we could learn from the Anangu and other First Nations communities to respect nature instead of trying to colonise and control it. We could live and travel purposefully, with appreciation and engagement rather than the desire for domination and extraction.

Nadia's trip to Uluru was also life-changing. Surveying the desert was awe-inspiring. For a girl born and raised in Sydney – a busy and self-important city of five million – it was an axis shift.

'Living so far away in Sydney, you stop and think, "Is this Australia!?" I thought, we need to get out more inside our own country and learn about our history. It's humbling.'

For Nadia, the idea of climbing Uluru felt as wrong as wearing shoes in a mosque. She found it hard to believe anyone would go against the posted signs requesting visitors not to climb Uluru. She was relieved when an official ban on climbing Uluru was finally put in

place. 'I just remember thinking, why do some people find it so hard to accept not doing something if a group of other people ask you not to do so out of respect for their culture or religion?'

'As a Muslim, you grow up with an understanding of sacredness. That not everything needs to be touched and experienced, whether that's not handling the Quran if your hands are not clean or not stepping into a mosque to pray with shoes. When you have that awareness, it makes you more open when other people ask you to respect their boundaries with how you engage in their space.'

Whether it's visiting a sacred site like Uluru or a religious pilgrimage, or a more spiritual experience in nature, travel can be a portal into transcendence. It can allow us moments of reflection as we interrupt the everyday to pay attention and go within.

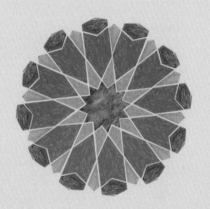

Sarah's Tips for Travel

* Make sure you have travel insurance, which covers you for necessary evacuation in case of severe accident or illness.

* Wear sturdy covered shoes and clothing, appropriate for the activity you are undertaking.

* Be careful in traffic; and follow guidance on safety rules.

A Final Word ...

I hope this book encourages you to live and journey with wonder.

It's my hope that you take away these collections of stories, tips and interviews to buoy and inspire you.

I hope they help you navigate moving through the world in a way that is joyful, fun, safe, inclusive and respectful. Sometimes travel comes with challenges; there is a comfort in knowing that we are not alone in these stresses and that no journey is perfect. There are times when you might get sick abroad, or lost, or lose your luggage, or end up on the wrong train with the wrong travel buddy — and that's okay!

I want you to see yourself in travel stories, through people whose lives and experiences mirror yours. I hope these stories inspire confidence and offers the potential for insight, transformation and making a difference in the world.

Happy journeying!

About the Author

Sarah Malik is a Walkley award-winning Australian investigative journalist, an author, writer and presenter.

An avid traveller, she has lived in Jordan and slept under the desert stars in a Bedouin camp, climbed Asia's highest peak, Mount Kinabalu, in Borneo and Malaysia, and travelled to over a dozen countries including Japan, Turkey, Palestine, Pakistan, India and much of Europe.

Her first book is a collection of memoir essays *Desi Girl: On Feminism, Race, Faith and Belonging*.

Acknowledgements

I would like to thank my family for all their support, but especially my sister Fatima who is my favourite travel buddy and whose musings inspired this book.

I would like to thank the Hardie Grant team and editors for commissioning this book and creating a space for these stories, and for all your hard work in helping bring this book to life.

I would also like to thank Yassmin Abdel-Magied, Aisha Al-Adawiya, Dr Susan Carland, Nora Musa, Raidah Shah Idil, Aliya Ahmad, Margari Aziza-Hill, Tasneem Chopra, Farah Celjo, Zenith Irfan, Nadia Jamal, Dr Umber Rind — your stories are a gift.

My neck stiffened and ⸻ returning to my
BODY. Different pa⸻ living parallel live
unds of artillery and r⸻ I used to climb the tr
and make paper dolls. ⸻ Memories have blurred.
leaped of their car and fle⸻ by orchard. All these year
taken in, put under, and woken up before I could worry much mo
People sniffed. There were black and white pictures of suffraget
hallucinated that Mum and Teta were living in a yellow tent on
We sat in a circle in a cluttered office. It reminded me of fre
cut lemons. We deserve to TAKE a DIGNIFIED STAND. Our law
could still make this huge scary thing smaller. Square-jawed
yellow-eyed, he was wearing his best suit. She's in the kitchen, i
slowly. I cant imagine that at all. We'd trodden over a lifetim
subtle frowns and bared teeth. They don't see PTSD as an excus
with our degrees and opinions, might have become 'too much'.
waited so long for an institution to say the words I needed to
hear. Two years of clenched muscle. You go from one waitin
space to another. The man stares at you like he can see
your insides. The question crystalises. Justice. Justice. Ju
'Smile please!' Hijabs and colourful dresses and
sisters who walk beside me.

About the Illustrator

Amani Haydar is an award-winning writer, visual artist, and advocate for women's health and safety based in Western Sydney. Amani's debut memoir *The Mother Wound* was awarded the 2022 Victorian Premier's Literary Award for Non-fiction, the 2022 ABIA Matt Richell Award for New Writer of the Year and the 2021 FBi Radio Sydney Music Art and Culture Award. Amani is a former Archibald Prize finalist with a visual arts practice closely intertwined with her writing practice.

In recognition of her advocacy against domestic violence, focusing on the needs and experiences of victims in the Australian legal system and Muslim women in Australia, Amani received the 2021 UTS Faculty of Law Alumni Award and was named Local Woman of the Year for Bankstown at the 2020 NSW Premier's Woman of the Year Awards.

Published in 2022 by Hardie Grant Explore,
an imprint of Hardie Grant Publishing

Hardie Grant Explore (Melbourne)
Wurundjeri Country
Building 1, 658 Church Street
Richmond, Victoria 3121

Hardie Grant Explore (Sydney)
Gadigal Country
Level 7, 45 Jones Street
Ultimo, NSW 2007

www.hardiegrant.com/au/explore

A catalogue record for this
book is available from the
National Library of Australia

Hardie Grant acknowledges the Traditional Owners of the Country on which we
work, the Wurundjeri People of the Kulin Nation and the Gadigal People of the Eora
Nation, and recognises their continuing connection to the land, waters and culture.
We pay our respects to their Elders past and present.

Safar: Muslim Women's Stories of Travel and Transformation
ISBN 9781741177763

10 9 8 7 6 5 4 3 2 1

Publisher
Melissa Kayser

Project editor
Amanda Louey

Editor
Sarosh Arif and Marisa Wikramanayake

Proofreader
Jenny Varghese

Design
Ola Haydar

Typesetting and prepress
Megan Ellis

Production coordinator
Jessica Harvie

Printed in China by LEO Paper Products LTD.

FSC
www.fsc.org
MIX
Paper from
responsible sources
FSC® C020056

The paper this book is printed on is certified against the Forest
Stewardship Council® Standards and other sources. FSC® promotes
environmentally responsible, socially beneficial and economically
viable management of the world's forests.